The Poems of
Charles O'Donnell, CSC

The Poems of Charles O'Donnell, CSC

✦

Edited by George Klawitter, CSC

iUniverse, Inc.
New York   Bloomington

The Poems of Charles O'Donnell, CSC

iUniverse books may be ordered through booksellers or by contacting:

iUniverse
1663 Liberty Drive
Bloomington, IN 47403
www.iuniverse.com
1-800-Authors (1-800-288-4677)

Because of the dynamic nature of the Internet, any Web addresses or links contained in this book may have changed since publication and may no longer be valid.

ISBN: 978-1-4502-4840-2 (sc)
ISBN: 978-1-4502-4844-0 (dj)
ISBN: 978-1-4502-4843-3 (ebk)

Library of Congress Control Number: 2010911492

Printed in the United States of America

iUniverse rev. date: 8/13/2010

for

Raymond-Jean Frontain

Table of Contents

Introduction

Born two miles northwest of Greenfield, Indiana, on November 15, 1884, Charles Leo O'Donnell spent most of his life in the Midwest. His father Neil, a native of Donegal, Ireland, was a farmer who moved the family to Kokomo, Indiana, when Charles was two. After graduating from the University of Notre Dame at the age of 26, Charles O'Donnell took his doctorate four years later at Catholic University, returning then to teach literature courses at Notre Dame. Within six years he was beginning to be recognized as a promising poet when his first volume of verse appeared in 1916. With the outbreak of World War I, O'Donnell became an army chaplain serving in Europe. In 1920 he was elected American provincial of the Congregation of Holy Cross, and six years later was named Assistant General of the entire Community. In 1928 he was named president of the University of Notre Dame and served in that capacity until his death six years later at age 49. He is buried at Notre Dame in the Community cemetery overlooking St. Joseph Lake in a row reserved for Holy Cross provincials. His World War I doughboy helmet was fashioned into a light fixture and hangs in the alcove of the "God, Country, Notre Dame" east entrance to Sacred Heart Basilica on the campus. In his tenure as president, the university saw some enrollment decline as a result of the Great Depression, but O'Donnell was an excellent fund raiser, bringing the university through financial crisis at the same time as he expanded its academic prestige.

O'Donnell's first book, *The Dead Musician and Other Poems*, published in 1916 by Laurence J. Gomme (New York) contains 121 pages divided into six sections: "The Dead Musician" (one poem), "A Hive of Song" (13 poems), "Dreams of Donegal" (26 poems), "Quatrains" (13 poems), "The Nativity" (a verse play), and "Odes" (5 poems). Some of these poems were reprinted in *Cloister and Other Poems*, published in 1922 by Macmillan. This later volume contains 31 new poems and 16 poems from the earlier volume. O'Donnell's final book, *A Rime of the Rood and other Poems*, appeared in 1928 (Longmans, Green) and contains 60 new poems (no reprints). When Charles Carey, CSC, edited the corpus for his 1942 edition, he added 49 poems, none of which had been published in book form by his uncle. Thus 199 O'Donnell poems had been collected by 1942.

To Carey's four sections of the O'Donnell poems, I have added four more sections. Section V contains poems that were published in various magazines (*Ave Maria, Lippincott's, Scribner's*) and newspapers but not included in Carey's 1942 edition. My Section VI contains manuscript poems found in the archives of the University of Notre Dame and the archives of the Indiana Province of Holy Cross Priests. All of the poems labeled "Fragments" (Section VII) are from the Indiana Province Archives. Some of these "fragment" poems were pulled from publication by O'Donnell himself ("The Bees," "Ad Dexteram," "Consummation"); a few are in typescript signed and/or edited by O'Donnell; and a few are in his hand with variant lines and revisions. For this set I have chosen a preferred text and occasionally include variant lines so that readers may select alternate readings. O'Donnell clearly finalized none of these "fragments." Finally, I have included Dubia (Section VIII), poems found among O'Donnell's papers but which may or may not be by O'Donnell. They are printed here by way of inclusiveness. Poets often keep manuscript or typescript copies of poems by other poets, to make up a kind of private miscellany. Scholars of early twentieth century American poetry may recognize some of these poems as being by hands other than the hand of Charles O'Donnell. I have chosen to end this edition with a charming letter written by O'Donnell to a nephew, a budding poet. The letter is filled with good sense and affords an interesting look not only at O'Donnell's aesthetic but also at his whimsical good humor. One is tempted to call the letter his Irish soul at work.

For the most part I have left O'Donnell's punctuation untouched, except in the matter of his idiosyncratic use of a double pause effected with a comma followed by a dash. In all these instances (there are many), I have retained the dash and eliminated the comma, preferring to keep the more dramatic of the pauses. O'Donnell's use of the comma elsewhere may at times seem suspect when he uses it instead of a full stop (period, semi-colon, colon), but I have left most of these commas untouched since their contexts seem to require a looser relationship between clauses than could be achieved with more conventional punctuation: O'Donnell wanted some ideas to be conjoined where today we would wish them more firmly separated. I have taken the liberty to remove capitals from beginnings of lines that do not start a sentence, in keeping with modern convention. I have added a line to "Homily at Matins" because a line is obviously missing in the 1942 text (its only printing) and no manuscript of the poem survives.

Reading these poems, one is apt to think of the lyrics of George Herbert rather than, for example, the religious lyrics of Alice Meynell, although the latter poet is more akin to O'Donnell's Mariology than Herbert could ever have been. There is evident in both Herbert and O'Donnell a sweet, almost naïve, sense of divinity that brings to their styles an eminent child-like dependence. Both men, of course, were priests and sacerdotal imagery as well as Biblical themes and scenes infuses many of their lyrics. Neither poet avoided the long form, and both mastered the sonnet. O'Donnell's sonnets are among his finest poems, the subjects handled deftly within the short form and his pacing often controlled by a fine sense of enjambment to keep his rhythm conversational.

O'Donnell deserves to be better known than he is. Many of his lyrics are so finely crafted they can rank with the best verses of his time. Some are touchstones: a delicate scent of Keats in "The Silver Birch," a gentle reminder of Villon in cancelled lines of "New Saints for Old." He spoke highly of Emily Dickinson before she was fashionable, and he brushed shoulders with important poets, hosting William Butler Yeats at Notre Dame, spending days with good friend Joyce Kilmer. He was at times an occasional poet, penning lyrics on the 1915 Panama-Pacific International Exposition and the consecration of Bishop Joseph Sarsfield Glass at Salt Lake City that same year, but these poems retain beauty in spite of their dated topicality. Some of his finest moments were reserved for tributes to the dead ("Said Alan Seeger unto Rupert Brooke," "The Dead Musician") and musing on natural beauty ("The Mountain," "Narcissus in Winter"). Embedded among all the religious poems are poems of simple human contact ("At Tivoli," "At Notre Dame") and poems that probe to deeper meanings than their surface readings at first suggest (e.g., "Assurance"). He celebrates the great ("The Spanish Stairs—Rome," "At Shakespeare's Tomb") and the not so great ("The Death Angel Speaks at Heaven's Gate," "A Hosting of the Gael"). He chronicles war ("Message from the Front," "Of Poets Who Died in the War"), and he muses on triumphs ("Immortality," "The Charted Skies"). Everywhere O'Donnell surprises a reader with fresh images and phrases: "sandaled with violets," "snowed over with the moonlight," "for Him men plow the desert," "I shall have nothing but my sorrow when judgment comes." These are the words of a significant voice who apprehends the world with new energy and can translate experience into language with easeful art. Some of his poems (e.g., "Partus Virginis") stun with such metaphysical splendor that a reader is forced to consider the lines repeatedly. We find a richness in his verse that continues to delight today, even if we sometimes have to mine that richness among the debris of a piety gone saccharine for modern taste. No matter—suspending disbelief can bring new O'Donnell readers hours of joy feeling the world as he felt it a century ago.

To finalize this project, I used a presidential grant from St. Edward's University for which award I thank President George Martin, Provost Sister Donna Jurick, SND, and Dean of Humanities Rev. Louis Brusatti. I reprint all the poems with the kind permission of the archives at the University of Notre Dame and the archives of the Indiana Province, Congregation of Holy Cross. For this research I was kindly assisted by William Kevin Cawley at the university archives and Christopher Kuhn, CSC, at the provincial archives. David Tyson, CSC, Provincial of the Indiana Province, kindly released copyright permission. Eric Trimble and Adam Pyles provided technical assistance at St. Edward's University.

Proem

In the Bread and in the Cup
wherein He is hid,
daily I lift Him up
as once the Cross did.

There is nothing in me
apart from Him—
I am only a tree,
root, trunk, and limb.

Oh, pause and see, now,
you who pass by the road—
you may pluck from my bough
the bloom that is God!

I. The Dead Musician and Other Poems [1916]

The Dead Musician

In memory of Brother Basil, organist for half a century at Notre Dame.

He was the player and the played upon,
he was the actor and the acted on,
artist, and yet himself a substance wrought;
God played on him as he upon the keys,
moving his soul to mightiest melodies
of lowly serving, hid austerities,
and holy thought that our high dream outtops—
he was an organ where God kept the stops.
Naught, naught
of all he gave us came so wondrous clear
as that he sounded to the Master's ear.

Wedded he was to the immortal Three,
Poverty, Obedience and Chastity,
and in a fourth he found them all expressed,
for him all gathered were in Music's breast,
and in God's house
he took her for his spouse—
high union that the world's eye never scans
nor world's way knows.
Not any penny of applauding hands
he caught, nor would have caught,
not any thought
save to obey
Obedience that bade him play,

and for his bride
to have none else beside,
that both might keep unflecked their virgin snows.

Yet by our God's great law
such marriage issue saw,
as they who cast away may keep,
who sow not reap.
In Chastity entombed
his manhood bloomed,
and children not of earth
had spotless birth.
With might unmortal was he strong
that he begot
of what was not,
within the barren womb of silence, song.
Yes, many sons he had
to make his sole heart glad—
romping the boundless meadows of the air,
skipping the cloudy hills, and climbing bold
the heavens' nightly stairs of starry gold,
nay winning heaven's door
to mingle evermore
with deathless troops of angel harmony.
He filled the house of God
with servants at his nod,
a music-host of moving pageantry,
lo, this a priest, and that an acolyte:
ah, such we name aright
creative art,
to body forth love slumbering in the heart . . .
fools, they who pity him,
imagine dim
days that the world's glare brightens not.
Until the seraphim
shake from their flashing hair
lightnings, and weave serpents there,
his days we reckon fair. . . .

Yet more he had than this;
lord of the liberative kiss,

2

to own, and yet refrain,
to hold his hand in rein.
High continence of his high power
that turns from virtue's very flower,
in loss of that elected pain
a greater prize to gain.
As one who long had put wine by
would now himself deny
water, and thirsting die.
So, sometimes he was idle at the keys,
pale fingers on the aged ivories;
then, like a prisoned bird,
music was seen, not heard,
then were his quivering hands most strong
with blood of the repressed song—
a fruitful barrenness. Oh, where,
out of angelic air,
this side the heavens' spheres
such sight to start and hinder tears.
Who knows, perhaps while silence throbbed
he heard the De Profundis sobbed
by his own organ at his bier today—
it is the saints' anticipative way,
he knew both hand and ear were clay.
That was one thought
never is music wrought,
for silence only could that truth convey.

Widowed of him, his organ now is still,
his music-children fled, their echoing feet yet fill
the blue, far reaches of the vaulted nave,
the heart that sired them, pulseless in the grave.
Only the song he made is hushed, his soul,
responsive to God's touch, in His control
elsewhere shall tune the termless ecstasy
of one who all his life kept here
an alien ear,
homesick for harpings of eternity.

Immortality

I shall go down as the sun goes
over the rim of the world—
will there be quiet around me,
as of sunset banners furled?

I shall take flight as a bird wings
into the infinite blue—
what if my song come ringing
down through the stars and the dew?

I shall mount, strong as the promise
forged in love's white, first fire—
a soul through the rustling darkness
on pinions of desire.

The Sign

Blossom by blossom the spring begins. —Swinburne

Not leaf by leaf the altered woodlands lose
the summer's glory, lingering overlong,
but bird by bird whose flight the wood-way strews
with silence, fallen foliage of song.

And spring begins not thus, O singing mouth,
blossom by blossom, the trees yet being dumb—
but rather say, when wings flash from the south
carol by carol the spring is come.

The Earth-Hour

The earth was made in twilight, and the hour
of blending dusk and dew is still her own,
soft as it comes with promise and with power
of folded heavens, lately sunset-blown.

Then we who know the bitter breath of earth,
who hold her every rapture for a pain,
yet leave the travail of celestial birth
to wipe our tears upon the dusk again.

But vain: the spirit takes, in sovereign mood,
a sure revenge, as in some tree apart
a whippoorwill sets trembling all the wood—
the silence mends more quickly than the heart.

The Poet's Bread

Morn offers him her flasked light
that he may slake his thirst of soul,
and for his hungry heart will Night
her wonder-cloth of stars outroll.

However fortune goes or comes
he has his daily certain bread,
taking the heaven's starry crumbs,
and with a crust of sunset fed.

Forgiveness

Now God be thanked that roads are long and wide,
and four far havens in the scattered sky:
it would be hard to meet and pass you by.

And God be praised there is an end of pride,
and pity only has a word to say,
while memory grows dim as time grows gray.

For, God His word, I gave my best to you,
all that I had, the finer and the sweet
to make—a path for your unquiet feet.

Their track is on the life they trampled through;
such evil steps to leave such hallowing.
Now God be with them in their wandering.

A March Evening

Fail from the field the shouts of play,
while twilight falls like snow,
and overheard on their westering way
the silent swallows go.

But songs are brooding in the hush,
and green sleeps in the sod—
tomorrow you shall hear the rush
of life, come fresh from God.

O Twilight Hour

O twilight hour, you come and take my heart
with all your folded wings and colors flown
from all your folded flowers, silver grown—
O twilight hour, you come and take my heart.

Your feet have trod what alien, far ways,
on all the battlefields of time you came,
in many a bower you fell upon love's flame,
your feet have trod what wonderful sad ways.

Egypt has met you, and the crest of Rome
has bowed you homage with a vassal smile,
and shadowy kingdoms of the dreaming Nile;
Egypt has kissed you, Greece and faded Rome.

What prayers have fallen on your silver ear,
Franconian fields and Frison fiords among:
bells have bespoke you, weeping queens have sung:
the vespers of the world is in your ear.

Contented eyes have closed in your embrace.
Your seamless peace has covered wild alarms;
nurse of deep sleep, the gray zone of your arms
shall fold the waiting worlds in last embrace.

O twilight hour, you come and take my heart
and shake my soul with silent presagings;
I walk a lonely road, and no wind sings,
but come, O twilight hour, and take my heart.

Harvest Fields

I walked today through a clover meadow, mown
and sweet with dying bloom;
treading under my feet a glory fit to grace
a king's way, or his tomb:
acres of loveliness laid low, and dying
of numberless lives, only the winds sighing.

And I thought, as who does not of other fields,
flowered with unnumbered dead,
wondering how those kings, the flowers of grass,
hold up a regal head,
plan of closer cutting, redder harvest-making,
all the world sighing and its heart breaking.

Ver

Sandalled with violets, adown the breaking way
she cometh, misty-eyed with hopes of May;
the changing splendor of the morning skies
holds less of promise than her waiting eyes.

Across the black, ploughed fields her scarf of rain
in floating folds enwraps the leaping grain,
while 'neath the velvet press of her thin feet,
quickens to growth the yet unbladed wheat.

And as she dreameth, down the blue, far rills
rise windy banks of unborn daffodils—
soft! is it growing grass or young birds' call
lisping to her, the Mother of them all?

Drought

There is no clover, and the frustate bees,
abroad upon the fields and down the lane,
through all the forests of unflowered trees,
monotonously murmuring, complain.
Murmuring monotonous with wilding wings
that bear no blossomy burden nightly home—
for all their laboring, but idle things,
but builders of a barren honeycomb.
Thus it is now the summer of my dreams
when falls no drop of rain or quickening dew;
there are but sands where late were singing streams,
and dusty bareness where the sweet thyme grew:
the bees of all my thoughts are idle long,
there is no honey in the hive of song.

A Farewell

Forget me, and remember me, O heart!
Forget me for the dear delight of days
we walked together down fair, fragrant ways;
remember me for that I now depart.

For that I give our one sure hour of bliss
as venturing a distant promised peace,
give joy, for hope that joy may ne'er decrease—
reluctant heart, forget me not for this.

Nay, keep me in your fairest thoughts, my fair;
though all the sundering night be set to pain,
it shall be day when we two meet again,
in some far valley of the timeless air.

The Earth Mother

Her lap is full of dead; the tears
wash down her graying cheek;
unto her riven heart the years
no comfort speak.

She holds them close, the flowers, the leaves,
her yearly loved and dead;
the universal Rachel grieves
uncomforted.

On a Little Boy Who Died

You did not wait the spring
for burgeoning,
but ere the first flowers broke our sod
you blossomed at the feet of God.
I think there was that calling in your blood
long months, and we not understood.
For oft I remember, now that you are dead,
how often in the days that sped
with shout and play about you, you
withdrew
and for companion silence took
with a still look.
I noticed, standing by your side,
your eyes were wonder-wide
and you seemed listening, though my ear
no sound could hear.
Once on your quietness I broke;
as one that woke
from strange dreams, awed but mild,
you caught my words and smiled;
and though with ready speech
you spoke, I knew I could not reach
by any art
the late far-listening heart.
You were wooed gently, little one,

into the sun.
Death laid aside his awful state
lest you should fear this new playmate,
and led you off to playgrounds green
eye hath not seen.

Dante to Beatrice on Earth

It is come home to me in secret hour—
O thou who sharest of the soul in me,
and givest of thyself into my power
the very essence of the heart of thee—
we do in this commingling but rehearse,
with weary awkwardness of hands and feet,
and with what marrings of immortal verse,
a life that love forswore but makes complete.
This being so, O one of all my heart,
witness what turn of iron consequence
upon us comes: the woven hands must part,
and right and left must be an exit hence.
Love shall withdraw to be love evermore—
ring down the curtain, and the play give o'er.

For you and I are shadows of the Light,
we are but echoes of a perfect Song;
we hold dominion but as stars, in night,
our blended voices, are they ever strong?
What shall we say, whose struggle to pursue
a valorous role but bare escapes the sting
of shamed surrender, would the words come true
by Babylon's waters should we try to sing?
Hush, hush, O heart! The other side of sky
there is, believe it, love, a wondrous Hand
forever wiping eyes forever dry;
there are no willows growing in that land,
and never shall the lips of love be mute,
God making of our hearts a faultless lute.

There have been lovers since the stars were young;
we come upon a scene which time has worn;
there have been who their souls away have flung
and found them afterward, bruised all and torn.
Matching their mortal with a deathless thing,
the brave and beauteous spirit they have spurned,
risen unchanged, shall they have heart to sing,
burning forever as on earth they burned?
There in our heaven of unsundered bliss,
if any tears were left us to bestow,
should not the thought of their triumphless kiss
cause the sweet currents of old grief to flow?
Yet though tears burned the cheeks of their despair,
the hand of God shall not be busy there.

Inheritance

In Donegal, where old romance yet blows
o'er hill and hearth, the children in the blast
of storm hear cries and clashing arms of those
whose dreams were deeds, in Eire's living past.

And looking on the fields with clover spread
they never stop to pick the wind-stirred bloom;
those flowers might be the blood their fathers shed
now come to ruddy blossom on their tomb.

They look upon the lifted sea that flows
in mountains shoreward, breaks, and piles again;
the winds, they say, thus heap a cairn for those
who have God's acre in the unmarked main.

I never saw the fields those children see,
the fog-scarfed mountains, nor the hilly deep,
but share their every dream and memory—
only the age-long hates I can not keep.

For there they lie, my fathers and their foes,
as in one grave they wait the trumpet call;
o'er some the foam, o'er some the clover blows,
the while they're sleeping long in Donegal.

Lament of the Stolen Bride

Faery Child: Come, newly married bride.
—W. B. Yeats, The Land of Heart's Desire.

Go, thought of my heart, on the wings of the wind
o'er the green on the meadows wide,
by the deep dark woods, with the sea behind,
where the stars at anchor ride;
steal into the heart of my old true love
as he turns from the shining plough,
and tell with the voice of the home-come dove
of the hunger that's on me now.

Ochone, for the land that is far away,
and Shawn of the stout warm arms;
oh, better a world where the light is gray
and night is thick with alarms,
than forever the music's maddening beat
in the moonlit faery land,
than the ceaseless whir of the tripping feet
and the clasp of the bloodless hand.

E'en yet, when night is on fire with stars,
or dropping the silver day,
I can hear the fall of the pasture bars
and the lilt of his whistled lay.
Then shaken from me are the dreamers' charms,
my hand from the dancers' slips,
and the mother stands lonely with empty arms,
and the widow with hungering lips.

The Spell of Donegal

The hills of Donegal are green,
and blue the bending sky—
for sky and hills I have not seen
the holiest love have I.

There was my father born, and there
my mother's cheeks were red,
and blessed with sacred rite and prayer
sleep all my kindred dead.

Across the fields the storm clouds sweep,
the screaming sea-birds call,
and waiting mothers watch and weep
on the coast of Donegal.

Hundreds of leagues to west and more
my own loved country lies,
and I must seek its eastward shore
with seaward straining eyes.

Is it the legends of that isle
that hold my soul in thrall,
its awful splendor, mile on mile,
where thundering breakers fall?

Is it a spell of water-wraith
that thrills me through and through,
or spirit of my fathers' faith
that springs in me anew?

The hills of Donegal are green
and blue the sky above—
for sky and hills I have not seen
I keep the holiest love.

In Exile

A wind comes over my heart, Asthore,
with a shaking of silver wings,
from the green, far hills I shall see no more,
where your morning linnet sings.

There comes to me now, like a flutter of leaves,
the lilt of a tune and the tap of a shoe,
my heart at the memory throbs and grieves,
oh, the voice and the looks of you!

Over the wind-vexed, sobbing seas
my dream-faint eyes now stray;
I am borne by a lilt on the evening breeze
to a vanished Patrick's Day.

A Shrine of Donegal

Lough Derg, Lough Derg, how chant the waves along
thy solemn shores, and in the flowing air
drift murmurs of an unforgotten song
and of remembered prayer.

A land of sainted soil and hallowed sea,
round no more sacred isle the broad tide rolls,
Lough Derg, than where the waters compass thee,
crowned with thine aureoles.

For thee the print of Patrick's holy bones
blesses; and echoes of the centuries' feet
that moved along the penitential stones
in all thy winds are sweet.

Here came my fathers in their life's high day
in barefoot sorrow, but God knows the whole:
not for themselves they fasted, but to lay
up riches for my soul.

Great waters are between thy shores and me,
my feet upon thy strand may never stray,
but, O Lough Derg, the prayers they said on thee
fall on my need today.

Killybegs

The harbor lights of Killybegs
look out to an open sea,
where powder and wine in Spanish kegs
came over in 'ninety-three.

Red Hugh he was the chieftain bold,
and high his word in Spain,
where never a don his beads that told
but cursed the English main.

Grandee and Irish chief were one
to hate the apostate foe,
and all they did was justly done
to answer woe with woe.

For every Irish lass's eyes
downcast for English shame,
beneath the accusing Irish skies
goes down an English name.

For every bairn sadly born,
for old men wanton killed,
an English heart is fitly torn
and the wild blood fairly spilled.

A cross, I know, no sword, was raised
there by the man of God,
but Patrick's dead eyes must have blazed
under the outraged sod.

I am a man of peaceful palm,
the leaves of a book I turn:
think you these old tales leave me calm?
I blush, I weep, I burn.

My mother was born in Killybegs,
long after 'ninety-three;
and I bless the bursting Spanish kegs,
the harbor and the sea.

Prevision

I cannot tell what way the years will lead,
how hands may falter and how feet may bleed,
what deep contentment I shall have or need,
I cannot tell.

I do not know why the fleet early years
should shake me with surmise of future fears;
why golden suns set in a gloom of tears
I do not know.

I must not ask of winter winds that come
across the ground where men sleep cold and dumb,
if I shall rest there well—of my last home
I must not ask.

I shall not shrink, maybe I shall not dread,
when time has slowed my step and bowed my head,
to go away, to join the cloistered dead
I shall not shrink.

I shall have hope, in spite of heavy shame,
among God's pensioners to find my name—
in Him who for the strayed and lost ones came
I shall have hope.

Restoration

From these dead leaves the winds have caught
and on the brown earth fling,
yea, from their dust, new hosts shall rise
at the trumpet call of Spring.

Thus may the winds our ashes take,
but in that far dusk dim,
when God's eye hath burnt up the worlds,
this flesh shall stand with Him.

In the Night

The joyful heart is slow to sleep,
repose it does not crave;
but weary are the eyes that weep
by sick-bed or by grave.

I lay awake the livelong night,
by joy too much made glad;
but with the coming of the light
I found my heart more sad.

The wings of joy are light and fleet,
they pass and leave no trace;
deep prints are marked by sorrow's feet
upon the spirit's face.

But God can fill the hollows up
with undeparting peace,
and they who drain their sorrow's cup
know pain at last will cease.

The joyful heart, so slow to sleep,
may find its morning night—
the heavy eyes of those who weep
may never lose the light.

The Woof of Life

In the moth-hour's silver gloom
the Weaver at His loom
the quiet pattern of my life would trace
the grayness of the moth
He wove into the cloth,
and wrought thereon the red rose of your face.

The Wings of Rest

The marble door before Thy face
what is it but a little dust?
The chalice, golden, rubied vase,
will drop away as all things must.

Thus fleeting are the things of sense,
Thyself alone eternal art;
not more the universe immense
Thy home, than any human heart.

In this dim room the tides of time
are changed and ever changing still;
here while the hour-bells steady chime
works out serene Thy timeless will.

I stand before Thee but a space,
if faith be seeing, sight is dim—
to sinners mercy show, Thy face
for sunset eyes of seraphim.

And they, my friends, who travel far,
they do not leave me, for with Thee
distance is not, and every star
whirls round Thy finger ceaselessly.

Requital

If lips with olden memories
in heaven are sweet,
mine shall have burning ecstasies
that kissed His feet.

If lips grown gray with pain
in heaven are red,
then mine shall bloom again,
of life here bled.

If souls earth-emptied here
in heaven are filled,
O heart, then let thy fear
be stilled, be stilled.

Angels at Bethlehem

Now at length they look on Him,
unbeginning Awe—
Cherubim and Seraphim—
on the oaten straw.

Dost thou know, who dost not speak,
woman all benign,
they have come from far to seek
little Son of thine?

They have stored their gold and myrrh
ages who shall tell,
frankincense, since Lucifer
quenched his name in hell.

Thrones and Dominations, Powers,
trembling on that doom,
waited all the timeless hours
on thy nine months' womb.

Michael, Raphael, Gabriel,
in the stable dim,
come with ox and ass to dwell,
serving Elohim.

Christmas Carol

Lambs and little children,
gather two by two;
little Lamb and lowly Child
here is laid for you.
Come to Mary's tender Son,
worship all, and one by one.

Lights are on His forehead,
little children, see;
other stars shall burn there,
red as stars may be.
Guileless children, for us plead,
us for whom the Lamb must bleed.

Little lambs, all in a row,
lay your faces down
till the Lady Mary stoop
and touch you with her gown.
Little children, laugh and nod,
gamboling round the Lamb of God.

After Christmas

Snowed over with the moonlight,
or turning back the noon-light,
down through the grooves of space
earth swung its old, slow way.
But, thronging the rim of heaven,
angels from morn till even,
watched earth with reverent pace
silent its orbit trace,
cradle wherein God lay.

His Feet

The Babe is sleeping sweet,
the Mother bending low
above the folded feet—
the roads that they shall go!

By lake and little town,
by heading fields of corn,
the city, up and down,
noon and night and morn.

Dusk and dark and day,
in ministering free,
they walk the broad highway,
they tread the very sea.

Unfettered, tireless till—
with all their labor red—
they climb a weary hill,
their work consummated.

Consummated? Not so,
those shamed and shining feet
the Way forever show,
and make the going sweet.

The Son of Man

He lit the lily's lamp of snow
and fired the rose's sunset heart,
He timed the light's long ebb and flow
and drove the coursing winds apart.

He gathered armfuls of the dew
and shook it over earth again,
He spread the heaven's cloth of blue
and topped the fields with plenteous grain.

He turned the stars to minstrelsy
as twilight soft, as bird song wild,
Who learned beside His Mother's knee
His prayers like any other child.

The Poor Man of Galilee

Is He alone at birth
due garb denied,
when all the looms of earth
His power hath plied?

Must He go houseless too?
Birds are more blest;
'neath all the nightly dew
for Him no nest?

Beg of the wayside corn
His daily bread,
the running stream not scorn
with stooping head?

Till at the last His tree
should yield Him all,
bed, drink, and garment free,
the Blood, the gall.

For us as if to save
He is denied—
unto the last He gave,
lo, hands and side.

The Virgin Perfect

The lowly things were sweet to her,
the clover and the dew;
creation all seemed meet to her,
both violet and rue.

A simple, busy day was hers
within her garden dell;
the common, even way was hers,
but walked uncommon well.

Not that she heard, but kept the word,
in this her virtue lay;
she slept at night when slept the Word,
to slumber was to pray.

To St. Joseph

St. Joseph, when the day was done
and all your work put by,
you saw the stars come one by one
out in the violet sky.

You did not know the stars by name,
but there sat by your knee
One who had made the light and flame
and all things bright that be.

You heard with Him birds in the tree
twitter "Good-night" o'erhead—
the Maker of the world must see
His little ones to bed.

Then when the darkness settled round,
to Him your prayers were said;
no wonder that your sleep was ground
the angels loved to tread.

On a Picture of the Holy Family

One, His very Mother, she
holds the Child upon her knee—
Him the Second of the Three.

Unbegot ere time began,
truly God and truly Man,
infinite in finite span.

One, with lilies in his hand,
by the two is seen to stand—
was there ever aught so grand!

Thus, when Joseph's work was done,
sat the Mother and the Son—
unity and three in one.

Joseph's house is surely blest,
harboring such wondrous Guest—
oh, but what of Mary's breast!

What of her whose heart supplied
to His veins their crimson tide—
Word made Flesh within her side!

Draw the veil of heaven and see
where in heaven's height is she—
nearest to the Trinity.

And beside her very nigh,
on the other side of sky,
Joseph sure is standing by.

Christ, as though the Trinity
were not home enough for Thee,
ye are still a family.

The Baptist

Leaping for joy ere birth,
shalt have scant joy of earth;
a dying life soon dies,
thy head a strumpet's prize.

And yet above thy bier
an epitaph dost hear
that makes thy dead heart leap
with joy, all its long sleep.
What was the Poet's word
thy lonely spirit stirred?—
Hush, hymns of night and morn—
"Holiest of woman born."

Gethsemane

He entereth the Garden, lonely—
follow Him, O my soul!
He falleth, and lieth pronely—
down on thy face, my soul!
Angels are all anear Him,
yet is He lone, my soul;
demons no longer fear Him—
lo, how the red streams roll!
Only thy love can cheer Him:
tell Him I love Him, my soul.

Into the deep hell with Him,
follow Him, O my soul!
Horrors no words tell, with Him
drink of them deep, my soul.
Challenge the worlds for sorrow,
shoulder the weight, my soul;
woes of the ages borrow,
take of all suffering toll:
think not of rest tomorrow;
bleed with Him, O my soul!

The Mothers

Three mothers met that woeful day;
one as her dead Son pale, one gray
with grieving, and one red with shame:
all called upon one blessed Name.

One from the sorrow of the Cross,
one by the woe of kindred loss,
and one cried out in agony
from shadow of a blacker tree.

One gave the Nazarean birth,
one brought the pardoned thief to earth,
while of that hopeless one begot
was Judas the Iscariot.

Among His Own

(In a Children's Chapel)

He lives among His own, the children's God:
above and by and round Him hourly pass
their hurrying feet; down hall or stairs, a pause,
and in the hush outside a knee is bent
in silent adoration of the Guest.
The Guest? Ah, no! The very Host is He,
and they the dwellers in His mansioned Heart.
For them the day is full of work and play,
of ringing sounds, of mirth and little griefs
that brim a little soul; and they forget
the awful Presence, as the child forgets
His mother, when the day is very full—
forgets her in the mind, not in the will.
For though they come and go, and laugh and shout,
at nightfall, when the spirit's eyes are wide,
and conscience looks across the vanished hours,
they find, what all the day contented Him,
they have not left the path He'd have them tread;
His arms were 'neath them, and His voice was heard
in all the secret councils of their deeds.
And when they fall asleep they hold His hand.

Partus Virginis

Him whom, as mothers use,
I bosomed full tide,
I bore, King of the Jews,
and God, beside.

They speak of star and kings,
wondrous in Bethlehem,
and angels with great wings—
enough, of them.

What should my thoughts do
since the March weather,
and first God and I drew
breath together?

What should I think upon,
day or night tide,
since Elizabeth's son
knew, in her side—

but the coming of Another,
on His shoeless feet,
I, the budding earth, His Mother,
and my breast spring-sweet?

Was it night or day breaking?
Little I could spin,
who knew my veins making
robe He should die in.

Nazareth, or David's town,
it was equal to me;
straw, or eiderdown,
shepherds, royalty.

There were only He and I,
within, without me,
all the still sky
folded about me.

He came: we two apart;
and I thought Him dead
till He wailed, when my heart
broke, and joy bled.

Martha and Mary

When Light is dead, the busied Day
folds weary hands and glides away;
while Night outspreads her starry hair
upon His grave, and worships there.

In Winter

Like ghosts of birds, the flocking flakes
amid the leafless branches fly—
but ah, the song, what power remakes
of silence vanished minstrelsy?

Elevation

Throned in His Mother's arms,
Christ rests in slumber sweet;
except at God's right hand,
for Him no higher seat.

The Shamrock

Sprung from a vanished hour
of sun and shower,
you bore a people's faith,
a fadeless flower.

Reception

A Magdalen, the scarlet Day
knocked at Eve's convent bars;
comes Twilight, penitent in gray,
telling her beads, the stars.

The Son of God

The fount of Mary's joy
revealed now lies,
for lo, has not the Boy
His Father's eyes?

The Spendthrift

With grasping hand and heart of strife
he seeks the fame that briefly lingers,
and all the while the gold prize, life,
is slipping through his heedless fingers.

Two Children

Names do but mock you while they greet;
sweetness and light you are—
the light beyond all saying sweet,
the sweetness like a star.

Stars

The foolish virgins ye, your lamps
through all the waiting night ye trim,
but when the bridegroom Morn is nigh
ye wither at the kiss of him.

Life

Only one springtime for the sowing,
and one brief summer for the growing;
only one autumn for the reaping
of harvest for the winter's keeping.

Request

Lay lilies on dead innocence,
strew roses on the bier of love,
but let my grave of penitence
be sweet with violets above.

"Scourged and Crowned"

A regal sequence see:
Him whom His subjects loathed—
before He crowned should be—
they first with Purple clothed.

Raiment

The seamless cloak He wore
they kept, nor broke a thread:
His garb of flesh they tore
as if from shred to shred.

At Emmaus

They knew Him when He broke the bread:
was't by the accompanying word He said
which faith, though faltering, understands,
or wounded beauty of His hands?

The Nativity: A Miracle Play

Persons:
The Holy Family
Matthias
Rebecca
Their Infant Son
Shepherds
Angels

SCENE I
Bethlehem, the night of Christ's birth. Early evening, near the house of Matthias.
 Enter Joseph, leading an ass upon which the Virgin Mary is seated.

JOSEPH
A wind hath blown the heavens into flame
about us; earth is silver to our feet.
By night, by day, God's hand hath guided us,
pillar and cloud His firmament hath been
to bring us hither; this should be the town
of David, city of our sire.

MARY
Even so.

JOSEPH
Here where the unknowing workman left an arch
in the broad wall we pass; thus Israel's God
comes stooping to His own.

MARY
Whereto He leads

we can but follow now as ever, yet
methinks I hear, over the din of song
that beat about our temples all the way,
the night-song of a mother for her babe.
Hark!

[*Crooning on the wind.*]
Baby, sleep, my child;
deep the night hangs o'er thee.
High the wind and wild;
dreaming is before thee.
Come, come the happy slumber;
bright dreams be thine in number.
Ah, baby, on thy mother's breast
is sleep for thee, for thee is rest.

JOSEPH
Let us approach; the inn mayhap is far
and crowded by the mandates of our king.
[*He knocks at the door of the house.*]

MATTHIAS
[*Within.*] Who is it starts the peacefulness of night
with clamorous knocking?

JOSEPH
Two of David's house
come far, and weary; may we lodge tonight
beside thy hearth?

MATTHIAS
Mine house is all too strait
for mine own household. [*Opens the door.*]
Beggars and their beast,
begone.

REBECCA
Hush; houseless, in the night, with child.
Surely some room can still be made—

MATTHIAS
But no,
we are too poor. [*To Joseph.*] The inn is farther down
the road. [*Looks at Mary.*] And yet—and yet—
Good night.

[*Mary and Joseph turn sorrowfully away.*]

MARY
[*Looks at Rebecca.*] Good night.

REBECCA
Houseless, with child—O husband, call them back.

MATTHIAS
Peace, they will elsewhere shelter find and rest.

REBECCA.
[*Musing.*] Her eyes were like the pools of Hesebon
that mirrored her sad soul.

[*Their infant begins to weep.*]

MATTHIAS
Lo, here thy child
hath need of thee, and of thine every thought.

REBECCA
He sickens, yea, his eyes begin to blur.

MATTHIAS
His temples burn; it is some malady
of sudden, unknown power.

REBECCA
Give me the child;
fetch thee yon herbs medicinal and oil.

MATTHIAS
His eyes are fixed; how his bosom lifts!

REBECCA
O God of Jacob, leave us still our son.
[*The infant dies. There is much lamenting.*]

SCENE II
[*The stable. Midnight. Mary and Joseph, with shepherds and angels, adoring at the crib.*]

[*Chorus of angels.*]
From heaven He came,
the Eternal Flame,
to fire men's hearts
with Love's own darts,
to conquer sin
and mercy win
of God above.

Lo, in the straw—
near may ye draw,
for God is weak
that ye may speak—
the God of peace;
let earth's war cease—
toward men good will.

REBECCA
[*Without.*] God knows, God knows, my heart is bleeding sore;
my son had hardly come to months that knew
his mother's lips, his mother's face and voice;
warm with my kisses slept he, in an hour
cold in mine arms. But she, that pilgrim spouse,
in dewy deeps the trembling wistfulness
of hopes unfathomable—pleading eyes,
ye draw me from the shrouding of my babe,
for she hath need of me. [*Entering stable.*] What wondrous light,
what music is there here! The Mother, ah,
her Babe. O God, stop all the clocks of time
and never ring the passing of this hour!

JOSEPH
Woman, thou look'st upon the face of God.

REBECCA
I saw Him in His Mother's waiting eyes,
and I have come from mine own babe's stark form
with swaddling bands I never may need again.

MARY
The heart of Abraham is in thy breast.
(*Giving her the cloths that were around Jesus.*)
Lay these upon thine infant's quiet side,
sister, that hast this night befriended God.

SCENE III
*The flight. Night. Near the house of Matthias and Rebecca. Enter Joseph, leading
an ass upon which is seated Mary with the Child.*

JOSEPH.
Ye stars, that run before the winds of heaven,
hide in the frowning cliffs of mountainous cloud;
thou, planet, wimpled as a maid, with light,
tell not our steps; God's finger points us far;
the way is His who is the Way. [*Lullaby on the air.*]

MARY
Soft, listen!

REBECCA [*Within, singing.*]
Baby, sleep, my babe;
God's own night is o'er us.
Jesse's rod hath flowered;
heaven opes before us.
God sleeps as thou art sleeping,
while angels watch are keeping.
Sleep, sleep, until the songful dawn;
God's day is here, sin's night is gone.

MARY
Yet, ere another westering sun his way
hath crimsoned, earth shall lie in their blood washed,
the sons that sleep this night on mother breasts.

JOSEPH
This woman's child hath died that he may live,
romping forever in the fields of heaven.

[*They pass along. Singly the stars drop out. The moon meets a cloud. Rebecca's lullaby dies away in the darkness.*]

ODES

A Hosting of the Gael

Written for the presentation of the sword of Gen. Thomas Francis Meagher to the University of Notre Dame, which already possessed the flag of the Irish Brigade.

This is a marriage feast today,
a wished anniversary
of union and reunion; Emmet, Meagher, all
true sons of Irish blood for honor dead,
with lifted head,
hearken to this most jocund muster call;
their ships are on the sea—
from ancient Donegal
they come, from Kerry,
ah, and from Tipperary,
yea, rather, say
from Dublin to Cathay,
from Belgian battlefields, from Spain,
from snowed Saskatchewan, from Afric sand,
from Flodden Field, and Fontenoy,
from every field and every land,
come man and boy
to keep with us this day a sacred trust,
for the earth is starred with work of Irish brain
and rich with Irish dust.
Behold, of heroes hosting here today,
in the farthest fore
stand men whose eyes

are blue and gray
like Irish skies
and like the coats they wore.
No party festival of North or South
by us is kept,
and on our mouth
no vaunting of a single patriot name
to envied fame;
but in one man stands glorified the race.
Their brow we grace
with crown of laurel and with olive leaf,
and in proud grief
that has no tongue and keeps its tears unwept,
we greet the splendid host of Irish dead,
leaving their age-old shroud,
gaunt witnesses, a cloud,
by every wind increased,
ghostly battalions led by greater ghosts
that round us troop, with measured, noiseless tread—
O God of Hosts,
we bid them welcome to our marriage feast.

Should any answer come
whence stand they ranked and dumb?
A sudden thunder of a shout
their throats give out
as if these long dead bones
yet kept remembrance of old trumpet tones;
the dense, straight ranks are stirred
and rises one great word—
"Fredericksburg" is heard,
while comes this chorus forth:

"We are the men that followed, followed after
the sun-bright sword and the sea-bright flag,
with a faith in our hearts that rose like laughter
most in the straits where the craven lag;
we are the men no danger daunted,
following Freedom like a star,
hot after glory, honor-haunted,
with our flag of green and our sworded Meagher.

"We are the men and these our brothers
who held the heights and threw us back;
over them, too, these thousand others,
a green flag waved through the war cloud black.
And Fredericksburg is an open story,
it was Irish blood both sides outpoured,
for they, too, followed honor and glory,
a green flag theirs, but not our sword.

"And we are come from the peace of slumber,
nor North, nor South, by division sharp,
but Irish all, of that world-wide number
in all times mighty with sword and harp;
to lift once more, from the dust, our voices,
in one last cheer that may echo far—
Fredericksburg in the grave rejoices,
now the Flag of Green weds the Sword of Meagher."

So sang they, pale dead men,
risen from their cold dream
to follow still the Gleam;
and in their hollowed eyes
were what with mortals pass for tears
as after many years
they saw again the frayed and faded fold
that was their Cloth of the Field of Gold;
and a flash as of a star
when they saw the shining length
of the blade that in his strength
girt the dauntless Meagher.
Lo! flag and sword together pressed,
by all their eyes caressed.
Then like a breath of prayer
they melted on the air.

Learn we from these our dead
the meaning of this day,
and be not lightly led
from our fathers' way.
Not what our hands may hold—

few threads of green and gold
and storied steel—
not by these tokens may we feel
sons of our laurelled sires,
save that the same pure fires
burn all our souls within,
and heart to heart, the quick heart to the dead, be kin.
Keep we the Faith sword-bright
by day, by night,
our fathers' meed shall never suffer loss
but know increase.
The sword itself is likened to the cross
that is our peace.

Ode: For Indiana Day, Panama-Pacific International Exposition

Prelude—To California

Who saw thy sunrise, Woman of the West?
For, Empress of the lands of dying day,
with all time's sunsets buried in thy breast,
thou hadst such dawn as can not pass away:
to sing of that fair hour is there not one,
O Mistress of the mansions of the sun?
Not all unwarranted I come this day
which sees far-sundered strands
in their united waters joining hands
and cheek to cheek Atlantic to Pacific lay.
I of a State that has for tide
the coming and the going of the corn,
some borrowings of pride
bring to this jocund morn.
When down thy washen flanks the daylight broke
through ancient night, a newer life and law,
barefooted men in brown—
and earlier the blackgown—
the promise of a day that would not set
for thee bespoke,

and their life saw—
a glory that the world cannot forget—
the flowering and the fruitage of a toil
whose harvest was of hearts not less than wine and oil.
O Feet, that tread the purple grapes of day
until that wine
thy seas a thousand leagues incarnadine;
thou that hast kept, how many ages old,
the tollgates of the sun, and toll and gate are gold;
arms that thou holdest, prophet-like, on high
till in thy daily sky
a victory for the sun is writ in conquest flame—
seek not my passing name
but know
that even as those sons of long ago,
thine earliest-born, the vanward of thy sires,
who found and kept thy wilderness a rose,
far-blushing to Sierra's silvering snows—
that so am I,
molded and quickened by the selfsame fires,
minstrel and pilgrim of the sky,
whose singing were the night winds in the grass
which no one heeds,
except it were of more than mortal deeds,
and memories that shall not pass,
and men that cannot die.

Ode: Panama, the Mastery of Man

Text of the rolling years that who shall scan!
Handwriting of a day that knew no sun,
rich palimpsest, through whose full lines appear
the records of an earlier day fordone:
writing in stone, a future deed God wrought
and folded it away until the year
when, counting all our yesterdays as naught,
His creature, Man, partaking of His power,
should read that purpose, and set free the hour
which marks completion of His ancient plan.

For there has been a Workman great and good:
fathom on fathom laid He in the slime
the unbreached links that chain the world in one.
He made, and swung the pendulum of time,
white magic at His word grew gathered light;
what golden jungle could have laired the sun?
He saw the Day upon the brow of Night
lay the first kiss that trembled into stars—
here opening pleasances, there setting bars,
the Worker in His power's plenitude.

What lesser Being could have sired the sea
whose waters prove him nursling of the sky,
finding his cradle in the various earth,
the ocean's hollow or the cowslip's eye,
but ever passing up and down a stair—
procession of continual rebirth—
the silken ladder of the sunbeam's hair:
behold the sea, how hath the mothering moon
some lullaby for him that she doth croon
while slumbering his breast heaves peacefully.

Who zoned the worlds with greater worlds of air,
a trackless footing where the lightnings run,
the day's broad rampart and its rendezvous
since chaos first was raided by the sun—
titanic battles that have left no scar
on all the frontier of its quiet blue
where soar our winged ships: the sentry star
that sees them sudden rise, then disappear,
to all their challenging but answers, "Here
is empery that God may not forswear."

Not from the star-veined heavens comes our gold,
nor in the flashing skies is struck our fire.
Doth any field of sunset give us bread?
Swollen with pride and loud with vain desire,
of old men were who vowed assault on heaven,
threatening with trowelled hand the day-spring's head:
and Babel's very tongue is perished even,

the sun shines down a mockery of their pain
and there is laughter of them in the rain—
the earth is our inheritance, behold!

The earth that is the sister of the sea,
the earth that is the daughter of the stars,
the mother of the myriad race of men:
gaze with Columbus over ocean bars,
drink with Balboa in thy thirsting eye
the waters that he quaffed on Darien,
with them turn homeward, loaded with new sky:
catch, if thou mayest, the lightning of the gleam
that crowns their brow of continents a-dream,
and thou hast neighbored immortality.

Thy conquest is the taking of the world,
the world that is and cannot be but good
since God first looked upon His labors done.
Canst thou forget Whose awful Feet have stood
even as Man upon the strand of time?
The Orient He, but till the West is won,
the furthest footing of the utmost clime,
His message has a meaning and His law
compulsion of obedience and awe
in Whom the racial destiny is furled.

Westward and farther west till west is east,
the oar, the spur, the spade, the axe, the cross,
humanity and Christ move onward one.
And be it counted to mankind for loss
if on this day no word be said or sung
for him who took the highways of the sun,
a pilgrim scrip about his shoulders flung,
glad robber of the roads that lead to death,
who stole men's souls, unto his latest breath,
conquistador for God, the mission priest.

Ye men for whom our bannered song is flung,
whose muscles have a magic that the sea
and earth obey, yours is the conqueror's mind.
Ye are the sons of olden chivalry,

yea, ye are sons of that high lineage
whose records written in the rock ye find;
ye are the sons of Him, the Primal Mage
Whose might in yours has wrought till Panama
outrolls the latest workings of the Law,

Whose earliest deeds the stars of morning sung.
Then let the morning and the night as one,
let East and West and all the lands between
north worlds and south together find a voice
acclaiming what this day our eyes have seen.
Until the heavens are folded like a tent
will all the thoughts of coming time rejoice
our swords were into yeoman plowshares bent,
and while this year on half the nations fell
the lightnings and the cursing rains of hell,
the last great wonder of the world was done.

Postlude: To Indiana's Poet, James Whitcomb Riley

Lo, o'er the fields at home now sinks the sun,
and with the crickets' hum
the tinkling bells of cattle homeward come
familiar tell
the dim, tired land another day is done.
And my song pauses for a last farewell
to you, and greeting unto one
whose ears
have caught, how many happy years,
the murmurs of the music of our speech,
whose tongue
our simple days with kindred art has sung,
and kept a silence where no word could reach.
Him by whose Brandywine
first strayed in childhood days these feet of mine,
brother and friend,
I hail him as our State's sufficient pride
and give him part—

whose words, deep-springing from a people's heart,
home-gathered there abide—
in glories of a day that has its end,
as has at length the lingering song of one
who brought his dreams to thee, O City of the Sun!

II. Cloister and Other Poems [1922]

Cloister

"Show me your cloister," asks the Lady Poverty of the friars. And they, leading
   her to the summit of a hill, showed her the wide world, saying: "This is our
   cloister: O Lady Poverty!"

Well, that were a cloister: for its bars
long strips of sunset, and its roof the stars.

Four walls of sky, with corridors of air
leading to chapel, and God everywhere.

Earth beauteous and bare to lie upon,
lit by the little candle of the sun.

The wind gone daily sweeping like a broom—
for these vast hearts it was a narrow room.

Launcelot's Song

When I remember you there falls
a silence in my mind,
as after gusty intervals
settles the spent wind,
and a far voice in the stillness calls,
silver, and very kind.

Then I give over matching words
against an old despair,
and I know the sky would fill with birds,
with song would fill the air,
if you could see in broken shards
the life that was so fair.

You did not shatter it, but I
broke it into my hands;
wherefore my sky is a silent sky
and all lands twilight lands:
of pride that towered as heaven high
there is not one wall stands.

Return

The leaves beneath my feet shall blow
again upon their tree,
finding the way back that they know;
and streams, gone to the sea—
an upland harbor they shall reach
however far they flow,
furl and unfurl upon that beach
the white sails of the snow.

Transformation

I kept a beggar's hut till Love
knocked at my sullen door;
I knew not what a spirit then
footed that earthen floor.

No lights were in his tangled hair,
his bare feet bled with cold,
but all his frail hands chanced upon
flamed into sudden gold.

In Late Spring

Only today the maples start to wear
that look of inward burgeoning, and I feel
colors I see not in the naked air,
lance-keen, and with the little blue of steel.

No bud is forth nor green abroad and yet
air seems to wait with raiment for earth's flowers;
above these banks, haunt of the violet,
hover with purple scarves the tiring hours.

A Road of France

All day the carts go by along the road
that bear a regal though a sorry load.
Young pine trees, stripped of all except their crown
which in the trodden dust is trailing down.
Young kings, that knew the mountains and the stars,
dragged captive at the chariot wheels of Mars.
Alas, I think, while gazing upon these—
if this were but a sacrifice of trees!

On Indian Lake

Apple trees on a low hill
and the dead sun behind;
the water red and still;
no sound, no wind.

Sudden the booming flight
of coots upstirred;
overhead, in the early night,
the moon, white bird.

A Road of Ireland

From Killybegs to Ardara is seven Irish miles,
'tis there the blackbirds whistle and the mating cuckoos call,
beyond the fields the green sea glints, above the heaven smiles
on all the white boreens that thread the glens of Donegal.

Along the roads what feet have passed, could they but tell the story,
of ancient king and saint and bard, the roads have known them all;
Lough Dergh, Doon Well, Glen Columcille, the names are yet a glory,
'tis great ghosts in the gloaming remember Donegal.

The harbor slips of Killybegs glistened with Spanish sail
the days Spain ventured round the world and held the half in thrall
and Ardara has writ her name in the proud books of the Gael,
though sleep has fallen on them now in dream-lit Donegal.

Well, time will have its fling with dust, it is the changeless law,
but this I like to think of whatever may befall:
when she came up from Killybegs and he from Ardara
my father met my mother on the road, in Donegal.

The Porter

I am the porter of a little door,
a swinging wicket in the walls of sky.
I open and I close a light-latched door.

There was an ark whose sides were precious wood
and gold archangels guarded its pale store
of wind-blown manna from the desert days.
There was a bush which stood a flame of flowers
and its approach was barefoot sanctity,
nor Moses dared its red apocalypse.
There was an angel rolled a stone away
and Roman guards swooned in their futile steel
before a tomb that April filled with morn
when Peter, John, and Magdalen drew nigh
and Peter entered, almost overbold.

There was a womb that bowered Sharon's Rose
and One alone that garden ever knew,
Whose only gate none touched, not even God
Who trod that close, God walking there alone.

But I am a porter of a little door
no higher than a man's reach in the sky.
Peter he keeps the ponderous gates of heaven,
and right good toll he takes at that turnstile.
I let you in for nothing but for love
at the little door in the little house of God.

Martin of Tours

"As I today was wayfaring"—
Holy, Holy, Holy!—low—
said Christ in heaven's evening—
the Holies yet more hushed and slow—
"I met a knight upon the road;
a plumed charger he bestrode.

"He saw the beggar that was I—
Holy, Holy, Holy!—long—
head and foot one beggary—
Holy, Holy, Holy!—song—
one that shivered in the cold
while his horse trailed cloth of gold.

"Down he leaped, his sword outdrawn—
Holy, Holy, Holy!—swells—
cleaved his cloak, laid half upon—
Holy! now a peal of bells—
shoulders that the cross had spanned;
and I think he kissed My hand.

"Then he passed the road along,
Holy, Holy, Holy!—land—
caroling a knightly song—
Holy! in the face of God!
Yea, Father, by Thy sovereign name,
begging is a goodly game."

After Mass

I kiss my amice and fold it close,
remembering what Saint John
arriving at the sepulchre
wrote that he looked upon:
the napkin wrapped about Christ's head
folded and laid apart:
he saw this thing and wrote of it
who lay upon God's heart.

The Cross

When Christ went up the April roads
the winds of April wept,
but through the woodway's early buds
triumphant murmur swept:
"On every height while time shall be
shall shine the glory of a Tree."

The Paten

A little golden cradle
it waits for Mary's Son,
until my words give birth to Him,
each day's Expected One.

A radiant cross where broken
the unbloody Mystery lies—
love, be our soul's horizon,
faith, seal our useless eyes!

Myrrh

In Bedlem, of Jewry,
the Gentiles brought Thee myrrh:
in the breast of Mother Mary
was somewhat ailed her.

Frankincense for Priesthood,
gold for a King's head;
but what is this for Lambkin,
the myrrh of the dead?

It was all in Bedlem
they brought Him burial myrrh;
be easy, Mother Mary—
there shall come another:

she that of Magdala's street
shall carry her name,
yet of thy Son's feet
shall bear her lovely fame—

Wise Men came to Jewry,
and wise gifts brought they;
but a woman in a garden
shall throw her myrrh away.

A Rosary Molded of Rose Leaves

Could anything more lovely be
than is a rose-leaf rosary—

wherein a garden bows its head,
and folds its hands and prays, though dead?

A cloister close, where roses wear—
the world forsook—the veil of prayer.

Out of the grave of summer rise
these postulants of Paradise.

Roses that morning robed with white
go softly here in stoles of light.

Roses the heart of June has bled,
with deeper Passion here are red.

In raptures glorious enfolden,
the golden rose is yet more golden.

The shrouding mysteries they wear
but show their loveliness more fair.

Could anything so proper be
as is a rose-leaf rosary?

Roses that worshipped God an hour,
turned into prayers that are a flower.

Advent

Hush! Dost hear a calling, Juda,
like an infant's cry?
Juda, selling doves in market,
only hears the winds go by.

Hark! Dost hear a footfall beating,
or is it stir of wings?
Juda, busy tithing cummin,
does not hear these things.

Lo, is yon a new light breaking,
now the dark grows deep?
Juda, see, a star, a wonder—
Juda is asleep.

Prodigals

I saw this eve the wandering sun—
spent was his purse of gold—
sink at his father's door, fordone,
as the day grew old.

Then from within the western wall
such floods of glory spread—
"They keep," I thought, "high carnival
for one they held as dead."

And I thought of how Love's Prodigal
came home on bloodless feet
to His Father's house and festival
and the right-hand seat.

Orbit

Nothing so much is future as the past;
I may not see tomorrow,
but, unto joy or sorrow,
my yesterdays shall meet me at the last.

Beati Mortui

There was a dance of autumn leaves, of yellow leaves and red,
a bright and merry maze they spun in the November sky:
I marveled at the young delight of these "about to die,"
when I remembered—did one passing whisper?—they were dead.

Surrender

No longer on the western field contend
the rearguard of the sun, while massed and gray
the shadows like a silent rain descend
upon the smoldering ruins of the day.

The Julian Alps

The mists draw off the valley,
the mountain summits show—
a dark-robed fraticelli
they stand, with cowls of snow.

Magi

Three clouds of sunset gather with their gold:
what strange persuasion does the half-light bring!
Just now I thought they grew like camels, each
with purple slung, and carrying a king.

Sunset

A Magdalen, the scarlet Day,
knocks at Eve's convent wall;
they clothe her, penitent, in gray,
golden her shorn locks fall.

The Watchers

"Sleep now, and take your rest," the sad words mark:
but one holds commerce open-eyed with dark,
whose bartered kiss the Master's worn lips take,
and Peter scarce awake.

Bread and Wine

Passionis Tuoe Memoriam Reliquisti

Herod's Fool and Pilate's King,
purple cloths and white we bring:
cloak Thee in the pale wheat, hide
in clusters of the blue hillside.

Trelawney Lies by Shelley

In the English Cemetery, Rome.

Trelawney lies by Shelley, and one bed
of violets covers Keats and Severn, so
the friends who went life's way together know
no parting of the ways now they are dead.
Young Shelley, like a spirit, spoke and fled,
and Keats, before his youth began to blow;
Trelawney counted eighty winters' snow,
and eighty winters fell on Severn's head.
Yet here they lie, like poppies at one stroke
cut by the selfsame blade in the summer sun,
the poets, and the friends who heard their song,
believed and waited till the morning broke,
then told their candle that the night was done;
when Friendship in the daytide rested, strong.

Said Alan Seeger unto Rupert Brooke

Said Alan Seeger unto Rupert Brooke—
they walked by the banks of timeless asphodel
along which Acheron's dim waters fell
with soundless motion—"Wherever here we look,
brother, are faces that our glances took
for old familiars of that world where dwell
those that we knew before we came, through hell,
unto this peace. Familiar as a book
we conned in school is that Virgilian brow,
and one moves toward him with Pindaric grace.
See where they meet, twin shades, and that they bow
where blind eyes star an old man's wrinkled face."
And Rupert Brooke to Alan Seeger said,
"These are the immortals, we are but the dead."

The Mountain

We are bound in with vague fold upon fold
of mists that wrap our world. We have no skies.
You cannot measure here as the bird flies,
there is no outlet where the fog has rolled
its greyness over us; till, as day grows old
stirrings of wind wake hope, before light dies,
of the low grey lifting; then, to raptured eyes,
a mountain peak stands forth in the late sun's gold.
Beyond the mists that shorten life's due vision—
shadows that mask and blur reality,
where frustrate sense treads hopeless in the maze—
there are those fields that dreamers named Elysian,
eternity saints charted like a sea,
and God, when time is done, the Ancient of Days.

The Desert

There are no fallen leaves in the desert, this
is not that Vallombrosa of the brooks
sung by the poets in their numbered books.
It is a hag-land, under the blasting kiss
of a pitiless lover. If ever there was bliss
of youth and grace here, moving in bowered nooks—
fled now like finches when coarse-clapping rooks
invade their neighborhood of maple trees.
This was my sin-burned soul, this were my soul
only for earthquake of the sacraments
loosening great floods like torrents of the past
that swept my barrenness from pole to pole,
till ruin breaks in blossomed penitence
spring after sweet spring lovelier than the last.

The Poet

In the Office of the Blessed Virgin

Who but Jerome should quarry speech like stone,
granite on granite phrase superbly laid
till like a tower master hands have made
the whole stands upright to the stars, alone,
four-square and perfect. "Hail, God's Holy Throne,
Ark, Mountain, Palace, Dove," as, unafraid
words of wide meaning he has justly weighed
into proportion, color, line, and tone.
Jerome, in camel skins, in your dim cave,
with only—Ah!—the Scriptures to your hand,
water and bitter herbs, hair-shirted rest—
what darling singer of the ages gave
ever such beauty in a flower-crowned land
as with a stone you beat out of your breast!

Ballad of Saint Christopher

1
When from the eyes of the blind man
the seals of darkness broke,
he saw men walking, as trees, he said,
that was the word he spoke:
Well, of all God's men and trees, I think,
Christopher walked, an oak.

2
He towered like the forest giant
above a sheltered town,
his hair such a weight of foliage
as the summer has for crown,
and from a height of heaven
his eyes like stars looked down.

3
Looked down, for he sought through all the lands

the king who was kingliest;
and he laughed as he passed the princelings by
in his imperial quest—
only the greatest king of the world
should bend the oak's high crest.

4
So, the mightiest king he found, and served,
till once, in a darkened place,
the master lord drew back in dread
and shook with pale disgrace—
when the giant cried, "What ho! my liege,
the blood has quit thy face."

5
"There is a king," said the faltering prince,
"who is supreme monarch,
dominion of the night he holds
and power no boundaries mark."
Quoth the giant then, "At least this king
is not afraid of the dark."

6
"Farewell," he mocked as he turned and walked
with proud majestic frame
away from the stricken earthly king
and his accomplished shame,
to seek the lord of might abhorred,
the king of the blackened name.

7
And deep in the wood where the winter stood
and the great trees groaned and tossed,
the man was met by the Evil Prince,
the lord of all the lost,
and joined his might with Hell that night,
till they came to roads that crossed.

8
And there where counter highways
were met upon the ground,

the Prince of Hell down groveling fell,
the fearless in a swound;
and a wayside cross by the morning roads
the oath of the night unbound.

9
The giant turned once more away
from kings of high degree,
and laughed in his beard, "The thing he feared
was a feeble thing," said he;
"since time began is many a man
has hanged upon a tree."

10
"But this," and a voice behind him spoke,
a hermit out of the wood,
"He was not only man but God,
Who saved us by His Blood,
the King of all the kings of the world,
and died upon the Rood."

11
"Where is His court," the giant cried,
and his voice boomed like a drum.
"By yon stream side do thou abide
and tarry till He come."
"How shall I know this Mightiest One?"
But the holy man was dumb.

12
So the giant stopped at the river side
where wayfarers went by,
a bridgeless gap that travelers crossed
through waters plunging high,
and back and forth through the stream he went
as the boats of the ferry ply.

13
And page or knight, or queen or wight,
he bore them through the tide;
he dwelt in the homeless forest

by the swift river's side,
and safe on his towering shoulders
the kings of the earth might ride.

14
But unforgot was his quest of the king
his service should employ,
and though he served his fellowmen
and had therein a joy,
the kingliest king he waited for,
and one day came—a boy.

15
A boy, there was upon his brow
no sign of royal birth,
you would not dream he was a king,
His garb was nothing worth,
you would not think to see His hands
that they had made the earth.

16
The giant swung aloft the child
as light as thistle down;
he did not know the one he bore
had all the stars for crown,
and he said in jest to his little guest,
"Fear not, thou wilt not drown."

17
The child looked down, and his eyes were gray
as skies that have been blue:
the giant strode with easy strength,
but soon with laboring thew
as heavier, heavier at each step
the weight on his shoulder grew.

18
And before they reached the middle stream
where the deep water swirled,
the oak was bent, and his great crest bowed,
and the leaves of his pride were furled;

and the ancient tale was come to pass
that a giant bore the world.

19
And the man cried out as a forest groans
when the winter winds are wild:
"The weight of the world is on me now,
who art thou, awful child?"
As the giant swayed, fordone, dismayed,
it was the boy who smiled.

20
Such silence fell by wood and stream
when now the young child spoke
as kept the ancient skies before
the morning stars awoke,
such stillness as in paradise
the first lark broke:

21
"O you who seek the kingliest king,
or ever time begun
I sat by the side of Him and saw
the tideless waters run,
and on a day, as a child might play,
the world like a top I spun.

22
"O you who look for the lord of all,
behold your searching done,
for all the kings are feeble things
before the Eternal One;
in earth or sea is none like Me
Who am God's only Son.

23
"O know you then, most strong of men,
the tree is in the bud:
or ever you stood by the river side
to bear men through the flood,
I carried the world on My shoulders,

walking bloodless through My Blood.

24
"And when the woods are blown to buds
in the last of all the springs,
when gone at length is the oak tree's strength
and folded all the wings,
above the tide shall I abide,
the King of all the kings."

25
This was the word the giant heard
out of the shaken air,
and once again a light touch stirred
the tangles of his hair;
but when he reached the farther side
alone he found him there.

26
And the man grew old by the forest stream,
ever, as at the start,
ready by day or night to thrust
the plunging waves apart,
and whatever guest on his shoulders pressed,
he bore Christ in his heart.

27
There is a garden in a plot
where all the bird songs woke,
and it is walled with emerald
as one hath seen and spoke;
and there beside the Tree of Life,
stands Christopher, the oak.

III. A Rime of the Rood and Other Poems [1928]

A Rime of the Rood

1
A word of mystery is told
whose secret shall remain,
that the heart of happiness should ache
with hungering for pain.

2
That God in those years of silent
and sole eternity
should know Himself a homeless Man
dead on a wayside tree.

3
For in the mirror of His mind
all things that come to pass
are, from the mystery of man
to the miracle of grass.

4
Himself is the enigma
that from His triune tower
moves barefoot down those timeless coasts
to make and meet His hour.

5

Before the fallen princes
set the balefires of their doom,
God from His central stillness
moves to a Maiden's womb.

6

He sees when we can not foresee,
He does what we shall do,
and Rome is there, and its iron rule
and the unborn race of the Jew.

7

All in His everlastingness,
before His time began,
something there was that shook His world
and made Him man.

8

Not yet had swung the planets
no one was yet to name;
there was not king or country,
honor was not or shame.

9

Before a foot was on the earth
or any earth to tread,
God chose Himself a deathbed
and God was dead.

10

Then worlds were turned where woods might grow
with sap tides running free,
unnumbered cycles making
a tree for Him, a tree.

11

God, in His day that had no dawn,
visioned a fallen sky
against whose storm-stirred edges
Himself should hang and die.

12
And time came down to a little span
when men contrived these bars
known as a cross, esteemed a curse,
an insult to the stars.

13
The Roman, when he broke the back
of Jewry and its pride,
came with his legioned banners
and this thing at his side.

14
Straight as a Roman spear and strong
as a pine in the Norse wood,
the Roman brought the cross from Rome
and its omen was not good.

15
High on a hill or by the road
where all might see who pass,
"This is the way," the Roman said,
"we deal with Barrabas."

16
"And I, if I be lifted up"—
what infinite jest is this
on lips that had eternally
a foretaste of that bliss?

17
Before the star of Lucifer
fell, or Eden's loss,
God in those years of wonder
was in love with the Cross.

18
They can be trusted, wood and iron,
to do their hapless part,
under the brawn of the Roman arms
and the hate in the high priest's heart.

19
They fixed it firm in the blasted hill,
He looked and called it good,
as the hour that He had hurried to
struck in His Blood.

20
A turn of pain and darkness,
a space of tortured breath,
and every fiber of the wood
grows alive with His death.

21
An afternoon of April
fulfils the eternal plan
that evermore His men might say,
"Behold the Man!"

22
That evermore while sight shall be,
cross-bar and upright rod
shall bear to the eyes of all the world
the broken body of God.

23
This is that terrible garment
He could alone conceive—
a stiff red cloak of wood and iron
His hand nailed to His sleeve.

24
Who walked His worlds of wonder,
God of very God—
He will not move in the shoes of iron
wherewith He now is shod.

25
Men shall not say a hidden Heart
is His and doubt thereat—
a Roman spear and a Roman arm
have seen to that.

26
Fixed in an iron certainty
no power shall undo
God hangs, His own love story,
and this tale is true.

27
There he shall be till the worlds are gone,
in Manhood and Godhead,
He who so loved one little world,
love' and life's Giver, dead.

28
For Him men plow the desert,
furrow the foam for Him,
because for them He trained His eyes
beyond the Seraphim.

29
Because before there was anything
or anyone but He,
God for His own Name's glory
put His Name on the tree.

30
And when the trump of doom shall blow
to strike the living dumb,
the King in His beauty shall appear
and His Kingdom come.

31
Then shall the top of heaven
and the last deep be spanned
by the bridge the Roman soldiers built
with its sign in Pilate's hand.

32
A bridge, a throne, a doorway,
a banner, a reward,
adorable as no other thing:
the Cross of the Lord.

33
Ecce nunc in tenebris,
Crux est lumen lucis,
Semper in caelestibus,
Ecce lignum crucis!

Design for a House

In my love, I would build you a house.
Its north wall will be God,
its south wall will be God,
east and west you shall be walled with God.
You will need to fear no storms from the north,
your south wall will be a sunny wall.
Dawn will stand for you, a wall of ivory growing into gold,
your west wall will be a pearl, on fire.

Walk to the north wall forever, you will not reach it.
You will never stroke with your hands the arras that streams down the
    southern side;
run eastward, infinitely, dawn will be still beyond you,
and you will be footsore indeed before ever your travel stop at the starred
    west wall.

In my love I would give you liberty, confining you only in the Infinite,
I would wall you up in the beauty of God,
in the reach and range of God.

I can think of nothing better I could do for you
than build you a house, out of my love.

Questionnaire

What did you think of, Mary,
as He looked up from your breast?
I saw His eyes like stars
in the early evening west.

And when you bathed His limbs
in waters warm and sweet?
I loved Him, adorable, perfect
from head to perfect feet.

What waking vision stirred you
as He slept, small and weak?
For hours and hours I watched
the little curve of His cheek.

And when the first words came
at length from His learning lips?
I could feel my blood listening
down to my finger-tips.

On that amazing day
along the temple hall
He taught the Scribes, you thought?—
my Boy grows straight and talL

At Cana when your words
hurried His coming hour,
You saw?—I saw His hands,
beautiful, with power.

Oh, and when at the last
He was slain by the crowd?
Never of my dear Son
was I so fond, so proud.

Then, when His cheek to yours
lay lifeless and cold?
I thought how never now
would my Son grow old.

But, ah, on Easter morn
you had your heart's desire!
He came to me at dawn
and helped me with the fire.

Did you know that He was God?
from Gabriel's word, of course,
Alpha, Omega, of all
the End and the Source.

But, women of all the world
that ever children bore,
remember, He is my Son,
and human, forevermore.

In the Upper Room

What did you hear last night, your head on His breast there?
It was Peter in the dark supper-room
asking of John,
who with Mary, His Mother, was just returned
from burying Him.

I heard His Blood moving like an unborn child,
and His Heart crying.
I heard Him talking with His Father
and the Dove.
I heard an undertone as of the sea swinging, and a whispering at its center.
I listened, and all the sound
was a murmuring of names.
I heard my own name beating in His Blood,
and yours, Peter,
and all of you.
and I heard Judas,
and the names of all that have been
or shall be to the last day.
And it was His Blood was calling out these names,
and they possessed his Blood.

Did you hear my name?
asked a woman who was sitting at His Mother's feet.
I heard your name, Mary of Magdala, and it was like a storm at sea
and the waves racing.
I heard Peter's name,

and the sea broke, I thought, and ran over the world.
You heard then the name of Mary, His Mother, Peter said, quietly, as he wept
   there kneeling.
I did, and it was like the singing of winds, and they moving over an ocean
   of stars,
and every star like a hushed child sleeping.

Again Peter—
What of Iscariot?
I heard the tide come in, and I felt the tide go out,
And I saw a dead man washed up on the shore.

And then John fell to weeping, and no one there could comfort him but only
   Mary,
the Mother of Jesus, and he could tell them
no other word.

"In No Strange Land"

Not those who find Him here where once He trod
and "Adsum" answers yet if man but nod,
not these explorers are of hidden God.

So worn earth's footway to His dwelling-place,
so clear creation's window frames His face,
that dark itself is starry with His grace.

But ah! the country of His far estate
where mystery and wonder on Him wait,
they are the dauntless souls that penetrate!

With faith as sextant and with reason's lead,
who sail the infinite gulfs to that roadstead,
and in their flesh drink of the Dayspring's head!

Aquinas, who charted God as men the sea,
Thérèse, so sure of roses yet to be,
she pledged beforehand her eternity!

Ignatius and his daring crew of seven,
adventurous, sacked the celestial city even—
Francis was wounded on the walls of heaven!

These are explorers of the Continent,
sailors that plumbed a depthless Element
by time nor sense balked of their high intent.

To find Him here where still He walks our green?—
They found Him there where they had never been,
saw with their eyes that which eye hath not seen!

Marginals

Veronica, the twilight comes apace
to meet her lord, the sun, who goes to die:
behold, the wounded splendor of his face
staining her veil of sky.

Low in the tangled forest of the sky
the branching clouds an ancient doom prepare,
and soon, like Absalom, the sun will die,
hung by his golden hair.

Now darkness, like King David, walks the skies,
his crownless head is bowed with grief and years,
only the night winds hear his broken sighs,
only the stars are witness to his tears.

Conclusions

Petal by petal I plucked the stars from the rose of the sky,
like a swain in the garden of love playing an old, fond game—
"She loves me," he breathes with delight, "She loves me not," with a sigh,
as he strips the leaves from the rose to the music of her name.

Infinite Lover, my own, I have torn the heavens apart,
like rose-leaves piled at my feet the stars lie, numberless, vast;
Vesper and Venus and Mars have told their tale to my heart—
"He loves me" is always the first, "He loves me" is always the last.

Vesperal

Let not a day with the west wind blowing
witness my going:
I should be desolate, swept away
out of his wild, sweet day
and his sky, his flying sky.
Bid him delay a little yet
till dust has had time to forget.
Then let him come, his old imperious passion
twisting the grasses to his fashion
wherever one may lie.

Wonder

I have never been able to school my eyes
against young April's blue surprise,
though year by year I tell my heart
this spring our pulses shall not start
nor beauty take us unaware,
beauty that is the blue of air,
blue crocus and a bluebird's wing,
water, blue shadows, everything
the sky can lay a finger on,
blue twilight and the white blue dawn.
But every year in spite of this
stern blunting of the edge of bliss,
when April first with blue-veined feet,
in any wood, down any street
comes as I know that she must come,
my foolish heart beats like a drum,
my eyes, for all the tutoring years,
are faithless in their truant tears.

On Meeting a Lady

It was surprising, after all the years,
to see how very little you had lost
of all the things that made you, though one fears
you kept them somewhat to your cost.

To this sufficiency one had preferred
the faint uncertainties that lace a brow
existence puzzled; if you had been stirred
by life, you must be different now.

No pathos of surrender, and no pride
of winning have contributed their grace
to touch you; while the world has lived and died
no hint of this is in your face.

Only, intactness, a self-sheltered peace,
as if you would not let life have its say—
poorer, I think, I find you now for these,
the things you would not cast away.

The Charted Skies

Before you took the heavens at a bound—
young airman, with the star-winds in your hair—
you had precursors on the floods of air.
Those deeps no plummet made of man can sound
yielded a roadstead all the birds had found
out of creation's morning. Free and fair
their sails were spread or any mariner
with Viking triumph of the sky was crowned.
Spring after spring they tack into the gale,
the fleets of robins, bluebirds, flying north—
who marked the course that these armadas sail,
who bids their comings and their goings forth?
There where your wings break on resisting tides
the frail craft of the swallow dreaming rides.

Beatitude

Take no drug for sorrow, drain the cup
until you hold it bottom-up.

Know that pain's own bitter wine
is pain's only anodyne.

And of this truth your comfort make—
after all, your heart can break.

Resolution

Love, You have struck me straight, my Lord!
Past innocence, past guilt,
I carry in my soul the sword
You buried to the hilt.

And though to eyes in terrible pain
heaven and earth may reel,
for fear You may not strike again
I will not draw the steel.

At Tivoli

It was some villa, possibly Medici,
grey as its ghosts and colder than a tomb—
we entered from the sunlight and the sky
and wandered drearily from room to room.
If it were only ghosts of happy laughter
haunted the moldy silence, all were well,
but why should all that sometime beauty, after,
ache with an emptiness no words can tell!
Only one little ray of light came breaking
across the marble gloom, a joyous breath
to answer centuries of vague heart's aching
and turn to rose the dusty air of death:
standing before some poor god's sculptured form,
by chance I touched your hand, and found it warm.

Harvest

I shall have nothing but my sorrow
when judgment comes, whenever that may be,
no fruit, no flowers, no sheaves—myrrh only,
and bitter as the sea.

Shall He regard me with stern anger
finding what He shall find,
or look with eyes that understanding
pity makes blind?

I only know, there is nothing in my garden
that will grow, to the grave;
I shall bring Him at last only my sorrow,
all that my life could save.

Out of the Idyls

Good-by, beloved, the days of our undoing,
themselves undone, we face a finer morn
when we stand up with bitterness of ruing
to curse the day that ever we were born.
That blackness shall be fairer than this sun,
than all kind words that silence shall be dearer:
we shall not care what we shall come upon
who know each hour the end of all is nearer.

They were two dreamers, tangled in a vision
that looked one way—but what shall crush the heart?
Not any force of time's unspent derision,
Christ and His love shall break those bonds apart.
The Queen's grave pilgrims held a holy spot,
and there are those who pray to Launcelot.

Shalott

Nothing she made of morning's hush
or dayfall's gold surprise
where through her fields the river spread
with all its gathered skies.

What does this matter, what does that?
For all that the sages say,
an empty heart is an empty heart
and life is a long day.

Yet, in the convent near, I know,
one like la Vallière
lay, still a queen, on the sleepless stones,
and Love stroked her hair.

The Shed

I
Sweeter than honey and the honeycomb,
and fairer than the stars are after rain,
the young girl, in her anguish, far from home,
knocks at their midnight doors, and knocks in vain.
I think she would put out her eyes with weeping—
men die, they are not born, upon the street—
well, here a shed, with cattle dully sleeping,
angels of God, have pity on her, sweet.
He was so helpless, the good man beside her;
but who would be accomplished in this hour?
There was not really anything denied her.
Heaven and earth were powerless in her power.
And who would ask for Him a cradle golden,
That in her arms and on her breast was folden?

II
The legioned angels come at length, and sing,
come wondering shepherds with their tardy sheep,
and, later, star-led, king shall ride with king

to lay their grandeur where He lies asleep.
She would be patient in that hour of splendor,
as she was silent in her lonely grief—
the Mother is so wise, the Maid so tender,
and her good man believed beyond belief.
They two shall keep Him safe, the World's Desire,
and one, upon the breast that is the Lord's
shall die—not she; the dread years shall conspire
against her, and the edge of seven swords.
Ah, by the tears that blind my human eyes,
I shall not quit her feet in Paradise!

Song

Always I loved a baby,
a baby loved to hold.
See, I have stolen a Baby
out of the House of Gold.

I found in the Tower of Ivory
a Little One asleep.
I have carried Him down the mountain.
He is mine to keep.

His Mother is my Mother,
His Foster Father my friend,
and I shall have Him and love Him
world without end.

In Praesepio

Midnight, the moving stars
and running sands confess;
now God steps into time
from Everlastingness.

O small, O weak, O poor!
Where is He, Lord of Might?
This human Child is He,
even the Infinite.

Only the bleat of sheep
and breathing cattle heard—
that is enough of sound,
This is the Word.

Before a Crib

O simple hearts and glad,
O foolish, futile things!
What shepherds, overclad,
what solid-bearded Kings!
A plaster ox and ass,
a Child with eyes of glass,
paste attitudes of awe,
and nothing real but straw!

Ah, by the fields of wheat
garnered and winnowed,
so brought to this retreat,
to Bethlehem's House of Bread,
truly we know the worth
and worthlessness of earth,
the impotence, the pain
that strives to set again
that timeless midnight scene
when, two good folk between,
upon a manger bed
resting His crownless head,
God by His own wise plan
set out to be a Man!
Oh, by His helplessness
our own we here confess,
and scatter straws that show
what way the wind shall blow!

For now a little bell
tinkles afar and sweet:
it has a word to tell
of chaff and beaten Wheat
and Cup—oh, Golgotha!—
of gold, as pale as straw.

Le Repos en Egypte

Where Nile the desert drinks,
three travelers on their way
pause by a nameless sphinx
and rest at close of day.

There in the waste of sand
One lies with drooping lids,
the Child in whose small hand
nestle the pyramids.

Sentry

The wolf was at the door
of a house in Galilee,
the prowler that men know
and fear as Poverty.

And oftentimes the Child
crept from His cozy bed
to steal out in the cold
and stroke its hungry head.

"Be you to these," He spoke,
"a guard by night and day,
be My beloved prized
for what you keep away."

Remembrance

The women wept as down the road
they saw Him fall beneath His load,
but, I think, by eventide
their tears were dried.

One woman did not weep at all
though no one knows what she saw fall,
yet in her heart today, in heaven,
the swords are seven.

Compassion

She was not very old the day He died—
so young she was the night that gave Him birth—
but when the spear withdrew that pierced His side,
no one was quite so old in all the earth.

O Lady, for the tears that you have shed,
I would make a song as evening hushed and dim,
could you forget one hour that He is dead
and to your breast, a Baby, gather Him.

To Her

He that shall overcome, I will give him the morning star,
John wrote, on Patmos, to Thyatira church. O prize!
I will charge the gates of hell till dawn falls out of the skies,
if so be I come at last to lay where your white feet are
a battered armor, a shield, a sword and a broken song—
O Lady of light and love, beauty and mystery!
It does not matter at all what else may happen to me—
l shall win the Morning Star, though night be never so long.

Our Lady Passes

When down the street Our Lady went
no stir possessed the little town,
and yet the sun for this event
put on a golden gown.

Shopkeepers did not pause as sweet
their windows saw her pass,
but cobblestones thrilled to her feet
like daisies in the grass.

A blind-man at the corner asked
why were the airs, that day, like spring,
A deaf man in a doorway basked
and heard a robin sing.

The Spinner

Mary the Mother of Jesus,
a lady of high degree,
sat by her cottage spinning
in Nazareth of Galilee.

A light fell over her shoulder
as she sat in the plane-tree's shade,
while a delicate lace of shadows
the sun and the green leaves made.

Busy her foot on the treadle,
and her wheel busily whirled
as a Child looked out from the doorway,
a Child who had made the world.

Deftly she handled the distaff,
and happily whirred her wheel
as the Child came down from the doorway
and ran at her side to kneel.

"Mother," He said as He watched her
there while she sat and spun,
"some things are more fair than I dreamed them
the day that I made the sun.

"And you are My heart of all beauty,
My star of all seas, of all lands—"
"Hush, Child," whispered Mary His Mother,
her tears falling down on His hands.

Natura Mirante

Darkness stands open-eyed with wonder,
light has before not looked on such a thing,
earth grows no portent like, above or under
heaven is no such cause for marveling.
Go down the lengthened race of men and women
until your searching end in Paradise,
you will not find in history that is human
the miracle that here before us lies.

That anyone should be both Maid and Mother,
should keep what she would never cast away,
because the very need of being other
demanded that the very same she stay—
Ah, sense at this shall marvel till the doom—
time's one inviolate and fertile womb!

Saint Joseph

I
There is no syllable he ever said
stored for our happy hearing, not a word
of him who helped to keep the Word, is heard
in the treasured accents of the holy dead
and unforgotten. By angels visited,
he hearkened, speaking not—his soul was stirred
as never man's, as none his heart was spurred—
What could he say, that midnight, in the shed?

Great moments thronged his life: why, on a time,
before the high priest, clad with his ephod,
a Bride was for bestowal, none so sweet.
He saw the Mother of God: apart, sublime
and mute, he stood, until his very rod
broke into speech of lilies at her feet.

II
And yet I think I know one word he spoke,
I think I know the place, the very hour,
I know beneath what gently ministering power
the spikenard treasure of a lifetime broke
spilling its splendor, as waiting the last stroke
of time's reprieve and folding like a flower
tired hands, tired eyes, beside the Ivory Tower,
he left life's burden light, and its sweet yoke.

Evening was drawing dim on Nazareth
and Mary's hand lay lightly on his brow
who rested in the arms of the Crucified.
He smiled on Mary, then with his last breath
"Jesus," he whispered, and the Savior now
leaned down and kissed him. And so Joseph died.

The Carpenter

He was the man of action,
captain of industry,
and his soul was like a single pearl
lost in the sea.

He was up and doing
by daylight and by dark,
and the sheltered veins within him
sang like a lark.

He swung the adze, the hammer,
he paid the public tax,
and his heart burned like a candle
virginal, of wax.

Coming home at evening
he had his loaf and wine,
and he saw in a young Child's eyes
all the stars shine.

He read in a Woman's face
the sum of love and beauty,
as all the while he went about
doing his duty.

The shop he kept as carpenter
was swept by seraphim,
almost, the Son of God
was lackey to him.

An eagle on Patmos
soaring, saw and heard
the secret things that Joseph knew
who never said a word.

Most blessed, baffling man,
history's one sphinx—
it must be heaven is
what Joseph thinks.

Ecce Homo

Dear was the face you bent above at evening
when sleep had veiled His eyes in Nazareth,
and dearer still that face to your eyes closing
soft in your sleep of death.

But, oh! Saint Joseph, to us something fairer
this face, no line of which you would recall,
Whose awful beauty is that there is in it
no comeliness at all.

Address to the Crown

He made them and He called them good
as they had grown in the bramble wood,
long and glistening, green and brown
thorns that now in a woven crown
approached to clasp His stricken head,
as gently chiding them He said:
"Children, My Thorns, on the wild thorn tree
that were your proper place to be.
Along your woods young April goes
and sweet in the brake is the wind that blows.
Here indeed you have lost your skies;
why are you twisted circle-wise,
what do you here in the hands of men?"
And it seems the thorns gave answer then:
"You know, my Lord, it is not we
have left our place on the bramble tree,
but evil hearts that cry for Blood
have torn us away from the April wood.
There is a thing which men call sin,
we think it is this that drives us in:
with Blood above, and Blood below,
You know we would not have it so,
with Blood below, and Blood above,
believe it is a clasp of love
we take upon Your holy head,
forgive us living, and love us dead."
And He who had made them and called them good,
the long sharp thorns of the young spring wood,
He bowed His holy head to them
and went to His death in their diadem.

Consequences

It is important that you came and died:
You might have paid our debt in Nazareth
and gone away, and rested satisfied
to leave us our monopoly of death.

How should we lift a cradle up on high,
what cloud of heaven point to as Your bed?
We who can show this hill, against this sky,
where you were hanged, and all men saw You, dead.

Your cross commands the crossroads of the world,
Your death makes death a door that was a prison,
and, crowning wonder over all unfurled,
except You died, how could You be arisen?

Except You died, while horror smote the sun,
You had not said, of all Your words, this word—
"Father, forgive them!"—Lucifer, undone,
well might have wept, as lost in hell he heard.

Security

Outwit me, Lord, if ever hence
this unremembering brain
should urge these most inconstant feet
to quit Thy side again.

Be not too sure of me though death
still find me at Thy side—
let pain, Thy soldier, break my legs
before I shall have died.

And when at length this heart is stopped,
leave not a final chance,
but send some kind centurion,
an expert with the lance.

Coram Sanctissimo

Ah, Lazarus, who art indeed
that board at which the world is fed,
I cast before Thy Beggar's need
my heart, a crust of bread!

And for those lips that still are heard
to cry, "I thirst, who am the Vine"—
take, Lord, this song, and at Thy word
its water shall be wine!

Raiment [II]

The world is weaving His cloak
with threads drawn out of the sun,
the water, the earth, the air—
how is He garmented fair
in cloths that creation spun!
Seed in the furrowed soil,
vine on the tangled hill,
the flashing shuttles of light,
the looms of the day and the night
with texture of beauty fill.
Then a morning word is spoke
mating that lovely toil:
He is clothed in His white and His red
robes, that are wine, that are bread.

The Breviary

This is my country, and a pleasant land
of winter, spring, summer and autumn time,
four-winded and four-walled, a changing clime
lit by eternal stars, constantly fanned
by delicate breaths of Eden. I know who planned
this terrain like a garden, like a chime
of answering bells, who matched a golden rhyme
of earth and heaven in these volumes spanned.

League upon league I travel every year
and in the valley, on the mountain rim
in winter starlight, or the summer air
I meet great persons of the past and hear
David, Augustine, Bernard, ah! and Him
Who walks this world—that He has made—of prayer.

Subiaco

Who fled from beauty and the ways of men,
a lad of fourteen, strangely strong and wise,
who would not trust the daylight and the skies
but counted darkness in this mountain den
and three years' silence—to this difficult glen
his name draws thousands, and their reverent eyes
gaze at the bed of his austerities,
the hollowed rock—ah, Calvary! and then—

the broadcast wonder of the risen word,
chant and procession and the tongue of bells,
light on the hills, the wilderness arose:
his vibrant Pax the centuries have heard
out of the quiet of ten thousand cells,
Whitbys, Solesmes', Einsiedelns, Cassinos.

Saint Jerome

(The Picture by Ribera)

Because your heart was flesh and not a stone
you beat your breast with flint; a human fire
ran in your veins, therefore you lived alone,
with bread and water surfeiting desire.
You drove starved forces through the sharp attack
that wins the ultimate freedom—after all
what does one gain, a coward, turning back,
when in the thin vanguard the best men fall?

About you, passions like a surface itch
ran their weak riot, lives that could not hold
your torrents more than the dull country ditch
could keep the ocean, shriveled and were old.
Ribera has you, by what wizard's charm,
the listening eyes, the loose skin on your arm.

At Notre Dame

So well I love these woods I half believe
there is an intimate fellowship we share;
so many years we breathed the same brave air,
kept spring in common, and were one to grieve
summer's undoing, saw the fall bereave
us both of beauty, together learned to bear
the weight of winter—when I go otherwhere—
an unreturning journey—I would leave
some whisper of a song in these old oaks,
a footfall lingering till some distant summer
another singer down these paths may stray—
the destined one a golden future cloaks—
and he may love them, too, this graced newcomer,
and may remember that I passed this way.

Super Candelabrum

That old Saint Martin of the Roman road,
see what a candlestick upholds his flame!
Time has snuffed out how many a shining name
since first in the Gallic dark his taper glowed.
Under the bushel of the centuries
kings and fair princes sputtered out and died
but down the years, Martin of Tours will ride,
his half-coat, like a pennon, in the breeze.

There is a road straight into early France
that parts time like the cloak cut by the sword
a knight swung once, a stroke that leveled death.
Beside it tower the woods of old romance.
It finds at night the castle of my Lord,
and on the chart God made its name is Faith.

Narcissus in Winter

From day to day I watched your pale green sheath
lengthen along the stem, swell at the tip,
growing from watered pebbles underneath
and turning toward the light an eager lip,
while speculation, like a brooding bird,
sat on the mind that saw your leaves unfold—
by what sure magic were your powers stirred
just so much green and white, just so much gold!
And cunningly the dark befriended you,
time counted out his minutes one by one,
no matter if our skies were gray or blue,
you had your secret commerce with the sun.
Process itself turns beauty's very flower—
for birth, for death, One waited for His hour.

Misnomer

(With a "Spiritual Bouquet")

Fragrance and color and the form of flowers
pass with the hours,
as the seasons pass,
drift to the grass—
but these,
they do not die.
They are not roses, though the rose be sweet,
nor violets that kiss your feet,
not pansies, nor heartsease,
they are my prayers, my breath

borne to the sky
and Him who sits on high,
Whose fair assurance that the bruised reed
is safe from Him, with Him they plead
in love and fear,
in hope and faith,
life's length till death,
my dear.

To a Dweller of Galilee

You who encountered Him along the road
that led to your forever nameless town,
Him barefoot, travel-stains upon His gown,
while those rude fishermen beside Him strode
munching disputed corn—to your abode
you might have asked the wayworn Traveller down,
served Him, and won forevermore renown,
and all of us had reaped where you had sowed.

But you who saw Him pass, where were your eyes?
Were there no clean of heart in Galilee
whatever way He fared, however He trod,
that you should be deceived by His disguise?
That only His Mother and the few should see
beneath His brow the tell-tale eyes of God!

Tribute

What part has Caesar in that western flash
of gold along the sky's translucency?
In silver waters of the dawns that wash
the coasts of day, what part has he?

If I am taxed by law because I bask
in this pale beauty and in that strong splendor,
I stand upon the law, whose image ask,
and tribute unto God I render.

Ad Matrem, in Caelis

I can remember flowers at your hand,
summer and autumn, spring,
nor less when winter in our northern land
forbade your bird to sing—
geraniums in the dining room
for you would bloom.

Dear heart, in gardens of the ever fair
long summer of the saints,
I know you walk, unchanged, in a gentle air
where the breath of roses faints,
and no eyes are happier than your eyes
in Paradise.

And if beside you walk two saints of God,
I know what saints they are.
One would be Francis of the birds, who trod
those Umbrian ways afar,
and the other, bloom of time's last hour,
the Little Flower.

Assurance

Of my unanswered prayers this much I know,
into the kindlier skies of God they go.
Who would have bluebirds frozen in the snow?

So, from my bounded north, my leafless wood,
to summers of His far infinitude,
I send my thoughts to range, to perch, to brood.

And though from that long bourne, so dear, so dim,
they come not back to my low apple-limb,
the eyes that watch for them are fixed on Him.

The Nightingale

Penelope's lone art
is hers the day long,
to weave within her heart
a tapestry of song.

But in the remembering night
she tears it all to shreds,
fall through the wan starlight
the silver, broken threads.

Joy

I ask for only the leavings:
when the high saints have had their sup,
if there be dregs or lees, Lord,
give me the cup.

The Crown

Grapes from these thorns we gather
engrafted on the Vine—
pain's quick and purple fruitage,
the Blood that is our Wine.

"A Worm and No Man"

—Psalms

Prophetic of all days, that line:
I know Thee what Thou art—
blight of the World, O Divine
Worm, eating my heart.

Magdalen

She wiped His feet with her hair—O brave dishonor,
paid for by so much more than instant gold!
With eyes that matched her own He looked upon her
and said that evermore *this should be told!*

Autumn

Now, like a painted lady, dies the year
whose breast was summer and whose lips were spring—
the wind—false lover—only stops to fling
a few gold coins, dead leaves, beside her bier.

Process

The seed, Lord, falls on stony ground
which sun and rain can never bless—
until the soil is broken found—
who harvest fruitfulness.

Plow then the rock, and plow again,
that so some blade of good may start,
after the searching share of pain
has cut a furrow through my heart.

The Spanish Stairs—Rome

John Keats, if he were living, with sad eyes
might from his window view the Roman street
turned to a bank of flowers where his feet
wore the gray stones, as under alien skies
he fled familiar beauty. The vendor's cries,
laughter, and all the bloom that makes earth sweet
have filled this corner of his last retreat
with liberal loveliness that never dies.

Poor Keats, a cypress shade forever falls
above your unnamed grave by Severn's side,
no sound, no step, no scent—while rose and musk
rise to your window in these yellow walls,
and for memorial at eventide
three blind men fiddle in the gathering dusk.

A Chance Bouquet

Whoever put these flowers in my room
launched me a ship of dreams on which I ride
down gulf-streams past Madeira to the tide
Gibraltar fronts, past Elba's iron doom,
to spring and Italy—a world of bloom—
do you recall?—as wandering side by side
we left the others and the accomplished guide
and gathered memories in the spread perfume
that made the earth a garden: Caesar fell
here by this hyacinth; Francesca there—
a daffodil swaying in the young March air—
swooned to Paolo; by that lily's bell
Beatrice stood lovely in her long gold hair,
while in these violets Keats and Shelley dwell.

Sequence

The sequences of summer sweet with rain,
of winters and black beauty of the trees,
of spring, of fall, of ecstasy, of pain,
meadows and mountains, and the sands, the seas,
shadows that follow light, and loss on gain,
intolerable loneliness, and love's full hour,
effort that fails, achievement no less vain—
how is the heart wind-beaten like a flower
to rhythms of some universal plan,
now purposeless, now plain, to prove a man,
mostly a torture, till there comes a breath
which is the last of sequence, which is death.

At Shakespeare's Tomb

Standing at Shakespeare's grave I thought of doom,
multitudes moving in a whirl of cloud,
and one soul calm amid creation's crowd—
the lonely poet from this lowly tomb
risen unvexed: of ecstasy or gloom
no tremor plucking at his golden shroud,
silence, although the very dust is loud,
making about him there a little room.
How had he dreamed this passing of the world
while breath and brain could dream and there was song!
Give him a pen, before the scroll is furled,
who else shall write the ending fair and strong?—
None other, yet his marble lips are mute,
all time he sang—let others strike the lute.

The Presence of God (A Sonnet Sequence)

I   By His Power

So light the daisy lifts its yellow head
within the wonder that is summer morning,
so independently the flight is sped
of swallows, all our calculation scorning;
so rich the sea, and skies so starred with splendor,
while mountains tower sovereigns as of right,
who should suspect that, terrible or tender,
not one thing is but is within Thy sight!
Withdraw thy hand, the daisy's gold is dust,
the skies are vacant, and there are no skies,
no earth, no sea. Our strength in which we trust
is but the lending of Thy potencies.
For all creation like a brimming cup
Thy hand has made, Thy hand alone holds up.

II By His Promise

"I shall be with you," once He said, "all days,
until the world's no more." Twelve fishermen
who knew time's length as little as world's ways
answered for all His followers who then
were but that sprinkling of the mustard seed
lonely and lost in the wide-furrowed earth—
His vision reached to other days indeed,
the countless souls His word should bring to birth.
With us, O promised God, Thou art, Thy power
availing still to lift our hearts above
the commonness seen, savored, touched, and heard,
topping the glamour of all sense, Thy love.
Wherever we fare we walk as twelve with Thee
along the moon-paved shores of Galilee.

III Where Two or Three Are Gathered

Once there were two who walked to Emmaus
lost in sad converse, sad and very sweet,
as camest Thou to them, unseeing, thus
beside us falls the tread of wounded feet.
Where two or three are gathered in Thy Name,
morning and evening prayer, the Rosary,
Thou art with them, Thyself, the very same
Who spoke of things Apostles could not see.
Lord, we are dust, a sorry kinship keeping
with clay that dulls our ears, we scarcely hark
"Stay here, and watch," until Thou find us sleeping
as Peter slept, while Judas coined the dark.
Yet be Thou with us upon every way
and when death comes, life's Emmaus, with us stay.

IV   The Paraclete

The Upper Room is hushed and iron fear
shackles the heart that droops with lorn desire
when, sudden, Holy Spirit, Thou art here,
with banners and blown trumpets and with fire.
Cramped cradle to a giant, the dear room
instant becomes: Peter is out the door
striding to meet the glory of what doom,
to front the public world forevermore!
Not less than in that Pentecostal hour
with all its urgency to words and deeds,
Thou art the Paraclete today with power
and comfort reaching all our human needs.
Thou art with Peter in his papal Rome,
there is not any place but is Thy home.

V   In the Blessed Sacrament

This is My Body, unequivocal,
This is My Blood, were ever words so plain?
Take ye and eat, and of this drink ye all,
do this in memory of Me, again.
Thy Voice has spoken, and what wheat fields thrill,
what vineyards quicken at the word come to pass,
Ah, Josue, the very sun stands still,
perpetual morning making for the Mass!
Gold yet unmined shall gleam in chalices,
and men unborn shall ever lift them up,
while others go before Thee on their knees,
Who gavest Thy very Self for bread and sup.
Who keepest like a lover constant tryst
with Thy beloved in the Eucharist.

VI   By Grace in the Soul

There is a little lake I know, a bright
blue truthful mirror of the blue bright sky,
upon its breast green reeds, by day and night,
soft in its circling arm of waters lie.
I think those very reeds are we, and Thou
art that encircling element, Thy grace
flows round us, holds us, moves and feeds us now
in the long day that waits to see Thy face.
A flood less palpable than air, than thought,
reality invisible, but still
an essence out of very Being wrought
the soul's outreaching readiness to fill.
My little lake and every bosomed reed—
the lovely articles of a lovely creed.

VII   The Mystical Body

There is one Head of all things, Thou alone,
O many-membered God. Thy waters fall
upon the infant brow as dead as stone,
and lo, it turns a member mystical
of intimate Godhead. Hush, my very heart,
and be thou bowed, my sinful head, for shame,
never can any future burst apart
the bonds that seal thee with the Ineffable Name.
O body of me, a member of the Lord!
Are these my lips that lightly dealt with sin,
my coarse hands, busy at a common hoard,
my feet so cheaply moving out and in?
Nay, Christ lives in me, 'tis no longer I,
never such glory, such shame under the sky.

VIII   Envoy

I have struck my octave, seven notes that fall
like birds with broken pinions from the sky,
I have shot my golden quiver, an interval—
seven shafts at the sun—upon the grass they lie.
Seven ships I launched on the adventurous main,
seven lamps I lit and swung them with my hand—
the night is dark, my lanterns flare in vain,
and seven keels are broken in the sand.
Oh, who could see except with Patmos eyes,
or who could say but with the horns of thunder—
the Presence that but makes our earth and skies,
the word that is the secret core of wonder.
Forgive me, God, that with a simple heart
I count upon my fingers where Thou art.

IV. Manuscripts [1942]

Waterfalls

I am in love with mountain
waterfalls,
the virgin mothers
of manly rivers.
I hate the names
a silly, copperplate civilization
has pasted on them,
"Bridal Veil," "Silver String"—all labelled
merchandise to sell tourists.
Waterfalls
are persons, even personages.
How they cheapen mountains, these daring
light leapers from skyey crags,
mountains that stand like oxen, sterile,
saving their life to lose it. These
virgins that trust,
stake all
and leap
out of the parent arms of snow
into space,
taking the chance
of life, that life is
with, underneath, the Everlasting Arms,
to hunt and find
the breast of their repose,
the meadow's bosom where their broken life
flows in a rich fecundity
through mighty loins.
My lovely waterfalls,

you that were yesterday
young snow,
maidens,
now,
rivers that thrill the sea.

Resurrection

Of all the manifold me,
what shall the last trump raise
out of the earth or the sea,
at the end of the world's days?

Dimly, a child appears
remote in a star-eyed dawn,
a quick disease of years
grew, and the child was gone.

There was a boy who ran
free in far fields and wide,
the boy died into a man
when his mother died.

There was a friend who fell
dead at his dear friend's side,
when, on a breath of hell,
his dear friend lied.

Thus I must reckon death—
the snuffing of a flame,
delayed, the ultimate breath
of life, is but the name.

Out of this sepulcher
that I must cherish well,
which dust of all shall stir
answering Gabriel?

Song [II]

My heart as the song is light
your Mother used to croon
when You came to her arms at night
under an early moon.

She is the Morning Star.
You are the Sun in the sky.
I love You, I love You Who are
her Son, as even I.

Watchers

White pigeons walking along the stable thatch
that roofed the travelers at Bethlehem,
anxious, important, like sentries on the watch,
bring in my love to them.

White pigeons talking as back and forth you go,
with exquisite awareness that the Dove
shared your fond vigil over them below,
give them my love.

Joseph shall see you, white pigeons walking—
without Christ's caring no wing shall fall—
Mary shall hear you, white pigeons talking,
Christ loves us all.

Ambassador

(For a Feast of the Blessed Virgin)

I ask a favor of the Holy Ghost
Who lives with me: Lover and Paraclete.
There is a Lady whom I honor most
of all creation. At her sovereign feet

today is holiday. Archangels throng
the radiant reaches of the heavenly way,
all saints in glory give her glory's song,
and I must have more sure approach than they.
Leave me in utter darkness for a space—
the darkness of Your shadow not Your frown—
go to her, Courtier, with a courtier's grace,
and bending to the blue hem of her gown,
kiss it, and say, as only You can tell,
how well we love her, You and I, how well.

A Prayer Against Millstones

I am Judas. Hate me, curse me, in the day
kick me into cringing fear, ye who pass this way.

Hound me in the daylight till I slink from sight
so I shall try no villainy abroad at night.

Point me along the road the rattling limbs of each tree.
Tell me they wait and reach and bend to throttle me.

Make me a dog, my tongue in the dust of the street
never to lift my eyes from my Master's feet.

Thus may I close this mouth, these lips of Yea and Nay
for word that He has said He never can unsay.

In Passiontide

Darling, my Jesus, as You go the road
will no one ask You in to eat his bread?

O Broken Heart, beneath the cross' load,
who cares that soon You shall be more than dead—
Darling, my Jesus!

O Sufferer, my Lover, who am I
to chide and wonder, to complain of these?
Had they not hanged You in the open sky
I never should have sought You on my knees,
Miserere mei!

O dark thief, cursing on the left hand side,
Judas—God save us!—on your blacker tree,
lest you two when the pride of life has died
have something bitter-true to say to me—
God save me, Jesus!

It Was Said to Marpessa

You are so young, so willful, and so fine,
nothing can give your gallant spirit pause;
you take for granted homage and applause,
whom nothing tires and daunts, whom nothing awes.

You could not be expected to divide;
there is a worm that eats the heart of things;
winter is but a word—there are the springs,
the summers, sweet with song and soft with wings.

Foolish, and young, and dear, you shall be wise
and old indeed, and shall you still be dear?
Who shall remember then your lovely year,
or care, so many later springs are near?

Yet there shall be within my musing eyes,
which even now to you seem tired and old,
a power to quicken roses in the cold
gray of your cheeks, and dream your hair to gold.

The Immaculate

No one so richly was redeemed as I
who bore indeed no stain of Adam's fall,
though due to bear it as the due of all
and needing, therefore, that His Blood should buy
even my soul. Judge, then, what Calvary
of His own mind, within the inviolate wall
of His eternity, He climbed, what gall
of death impossible He drank to try
for this effect: that never body or soul
the least unloveliness ever should touch
of her whose blood should make His own veins blue.
Oh, you were bought by what incalculable dole,
but I—what secret price was paid, how much?
Only my Son knows as He always knew.

The Serpent

No one could know so well as He
what arms He filled,
how brimmed her cup's felicity
that should be spilled.

And if His Mother saw His eyes
unseal with tears,
how could she guess the future skies,
the coming years?

He knows the price He is to pay.
Life now can feel
what dear-bought triumph on a day
awaits her heel.

Waiting

Coming, coming, coming—wise
Joseph looks in Mary's eyes:
"I have got His cradle done"—
and her look to his replies,
dreaming of her little One—
"All my wool is spun."

Coming, coming, coming—Eve
was, alas! the first to weave
clothes against His coming, when,
angry with the race of men,
He came with lightning in His eyes
and shut the gates of paradise.

Atonement

I am afraid of my contrition, Lord, its tide
is salt and deep;
over the keels of hope, however fair they ride,
disasters sweep.
Nothing above the bridge but blackness that once
was air,
and nothing at all below but steep gulfs of despair.
I know Thy slightest act, being infinitely priced,
had saved my soul.
Thy Father had appeased, O infinite-suffering Christ:
I need the whole—
for just my peace, for hope that barely does not fail
I need the superfluous spear, Oh, God!
The last drop pale.

Sorrow with blinded eyes had shouldered me to hell
except for this,
a greater grief, a pain no words could ever tell—
a traitor's kiss—
had swept Thy soul, mounted and paid a price
that even for such as me adequately
must suffice.

Apologia

If ever curious watchers should surprise
tears in my haggard eyes—
as might be, if they took one unaware,
alone, when prayer is prayer—
or someone in my room when I am gone
idly should happen on
those hidden instruments, the tools of pain,
hair-shirt and scourge and chain;
or even, unacquainted with the whole
program that shapes the soul,
at all my days with lifted eyebrows glance,
at cloisters look askance,
scorning the worn soutane, the shaven head,
regard the living dead—
there is one only answer which, though plain,
is given still in vain,
one word that never has for them sufficed:
I am in love with Christ,
and all the more because in days apart
by sin I broke His Heart,
and He by love as human as divine
has utterly broken mine.
These things are hardly mentioned with good grace,
I know, in the market-place:
they are not altogether personal—
simply, one speaks for all.

Addolorata

I would not rob you of one sword you have,
carry them to the grave!
Should some hand seek to draw them, understand
it will not be my hand.

Exchange that stark pre-eminence of woe
for comfort? Lady, no.
Keep, keep those eyes, that brow, that heart, that face,
O Bravery of our race!

The Uncreated Beauty

The shadow of Your arms and of Your face
takes hold of me. Ah, God, it is unfair
Your beauty should invade our mortal air
to form a coalition of such grace
the heart is shook in its most secret place!
How can I miss You Who are everywhere!
Yet in this bright predicament I dare
make much of what is only beauty's trace.

Thrift, thrift, my Lord! Take back this glorious lending
wherewith by too much beauty sense is won,
leave me a darkened world, lest by this spending
at last, but half-way come, I fall undone—
a moth that in bewilderment unending
mistook a flickering candle for the sun.

The Priest to his Hands

Sometimes, I think, I scarcely know my hands
they are so busy moving to and fro
to the Trappists on retreat. It only stands
to reason they should soil and wear: commands,
entreaties, flatteries, the constant glow
of action, all these things in time, you know,
will tell on them, really they are in bands.

They should be free and spotless utterly
for this they have a guard of prayer and oil
and so great is their common destiny
there should not be expected any toil
of them more than there might of angels be,
veiling their faces as their sum of toil.

Therefore I love my hands and keep them clean
by so much as they were unclean before
the holy oils fell glistening on the skin.
Man-God Almighty chose Himself a Queen
drawing beforehand on her Son's great store,
He made her soul and body, free from sin.

Prayer for a Traveler

Father, Son and Paraclete,
Mary, Joseph, John,
guard your heart and guide your feet
now till set of sun.

Bring you to that family-seat
Christ for us has won—
Father, Son, and Paraclete,
Mary, Joseph, John!

The Passionate Lover

The travail of love is over and done,
I shall be dead before set of sun;
My Father Who missed Me
these thirty and three years as men reckon,
He calls Me now and His angels beckon—
Judas has kissed Me.

My Mother is here, the lines of her face
in a blur of beauty I yet can trace,
and John is beside Me.
Snug by the fire at a woman's nod,
Peter who knew I was Son of God,
Peter denied Me.

Yet, notwithstanding the shame and the pain
I would go through it all again
and Heaven approve Me,
I would leave My Father, bow My head,
take nails and spear, My whole life shed,
if you would love Me.

Mothers of Priests

All mothers stand by Mary as of right,
ranked by that loveliest prerogative
God out of His creative hand can give,
that they should share His rapture and His might
Who brooded over the worlds. In heaven's height
these valiant daughters of the timeless Eve,
who cast away to keep, who died to live,
all anguished past, have gathered all delight.

But you whose sons move among sanctities,
whose hands, whose lips, such potencies endow
as only they who are God's priests can know—
closest you are to her whose dreaming eyes
gazing in heaven on her Son's dear brow,
remember still on earth the long thorns grow.

Message from the Front

I
When I am dead, and the little hill of clay
lies heavy on a heart that was so light,
the sun will have his golden tryst with Day,
the stars their ancient dalliance with Night.
When I am deep compounded with the mold,
I shall not mind me of my prison bars.
I shall not envy all that game of gold
nor dream askance upon the happy stars.
Only if to my silent home should come—
by what dim roads—a murmur of your grief,

then speech should break from lips the dust makes dumb,
and pain more sharp than death should claim relief:
if you were sad, however dull I sleep,
I should awaken in the grave and weep.

II
Then do not grieve, but let my little word—
of selfsame import as great poets spoke,
kind Shakespeare and Christine Rosetti—be heard
when on my grave the April winds are woke.
I would detach myself from memory,
even such memory as most I prize,
that which your fondest fancy keeps of me
should that but set a shadow in your eyes.
Far were it dearer in the dust to find
oblivion than know the light were gone
out of your face, and for your sleepless mind
no comfort at the dayfall or at dawn.
So, fare you forth, under a laughing sky,
lead here a new love where these ashes lie.

III
I shall not stir, there will be only grass
waving and simple flowers at your feet,
few daisies bending in the winds that pass,
the winds that to the living are so sweet.
I shall not care, provided that you smile
not sadly as you read my lettered name,
your happiness but pausing a brief while
to yield me part in it I would not claim.
I should be comforted as here you stand
fast by another and should ask for naught
except more kindly he should keep your hand
through the long years, and I be all forgot.
Thus should I bid you if the dust gave breath—
and then address me to the second death.

Londonderry in an Evil Day

A sword for Hugh O'Donnell, a sword for Hugh O'Neill,
and princely horses prancing and dancing in the sun,
a strip of shining water, a kingly curved keel,
the old war is the new war till the old war is won.

The old war that never ceased though tried blades were shivered,
the old will that never failed though fine hearts broke,
the old cause the new cause to our hands delivered,
and our hands our father's hands, dealing stroke for stroke.

For there are men in Derry, and there is dust in Rome—
I hear Columba calling, the anointed of the Lord—
and the Princes of Tirconnell have turned their faces home,
the Red Hand of Ulster has drawn the red sword.

Lineage

"But for this sacrament of bread and wine
the race of David were extinct"—I heard
with some amazement this ingenious word—
"Here flows the living Blood of David's line,
and here alone." Yet so it is, the Vine,
still to the tips of all its branches stirred
with that dear life His Mother's veins conferred,
springs from his seed who slew the Philistine.

So when the bells tinkle to tell He comes
to find His lost sheep be they far or near,
and the shed silence with His presence fills—
a peal of trumpets and a roll of drums
for royalty—yet in the hush I hear
a shepherd piping in the lonely hills.

A Letter to a Lady

My Dear, Our Lady of Lourdes
you are to me
almost a distinct person
since I visited your shrine
at Lourdes.
Still, you have been so long
my Mother, my heart's delight, the most wonderful,
the most beautiful
person of all God's making—
except your Son for whom God made you finest and fairest—
that even now,
after Lourdes,
I come to you with some homely clatter
of a child's footsteps
asking you to mend, perhaps,
a broken toy.

Joseph Speaks

A music murmuring in my brain,
the Name of Names I kept
from that far night when in my pain
that slept not when I slept
an angel of God His secret spoke
and I awoke.

Oh, falling like a waterfall
or booming like the sea
at work, at meat, at prayer—in all
that Name companioned me
unutterably.

I laid the Name upon Him, I
who little else have spoken
when first His Blood was spilled and nigh
His Mother's heart was broken
at Simeon's token.

Homily for Matins

What is all this noise that the sparrows are making?
I am late with my crumbs at the window-sill.
Snow is over all, and the day past breaking—
never fear, my sparrows, you shall have your fill.

Once I thought you greedy, and quarrelsome, and dirty.
[But I have come to love your springtime song.]
At forty one is wiser than one was at thirty.
I have learned, among other things, the winters are long.

The life that is hidden in your absurd feathers
comes even from Him we name upon our knees,
Who watches over sparrows, in all winds and weathers,
and said for our comfort we were more than these.

My vision of you is rather a revision:
patronizing past, I no longer discuss
your looks or your manners—with forgivable precision
you might remark they reminded God of us.

Destiny

One shall be taken and another left—
the stacked sheaves wait in wonder;
even a little of that hope had cleft
my heart, I think, asunder.

Here in an August calm of sun they see
the end that shaped the sowing—
which shall be bread and which of all shall be
His flesh, there is no knowing.

Confession

He talked with sinners, ate with them, and died
with two for company on the sorry hill,
and when gray dawns have brought us to His side
we know, heart-brokenly, He loves us still.

Commentary

By reassembling the vibrations, still extant in the air, some day science may actually be able to reproduce any sound of the past, for example, the Gettysburg Address, or even the Sermon on the Mount. —News Item.

I shall wait patiently. To sunder
from thrice ten trillion words one word!
Was it His voice, or was it thunder?
They did not know who heard.

But if one word should be recaptured—
One of all time's loud history—
Fetch me the Maiden's young, enraptured
"Ecce ancilla Domini."

The Promise

This day, with Me, in Paradise—
three hours the robber hung
with heaven in his adoring eyes
and hell about him flung.
He heard the cry of the Great Dead,
yet death came not to bow his head.

The searching spear he first must see
open the quiet side,
and his own body broken be
before he knew he died
by the still, sweet places where he woke
and the remembered Voice that spoke.

This day, with Me, in Paradise,
three words for three long hours
of stricken earth, of shattered skies,
triumphant evil powers.
But when he woke, as when he died,
there was One waiting by his side.

The Quest

You are my torture, Beauty: hands
that approach, unfathomable eyes;
citizen of all enchanted lands
bright with a thousand skies.
And yet how can I for your sake unsay
the inexorable words, keep what is cast away?

Revision

The temple veil is rent, the rocks are riven,
God speaks: "To Us this day a Son is given"—
that happy scripture of His hallowed birth
we trace in Blood upon the trembling earth.

Ruth

I am that Moab wife who chose
an alien land of free accord:
see if my name be not with those
that reared the lineage of the Lord.

Saint Agnes

Juda's Lion, like a lamb,
before His shearers stood,
and Agnes, like a lion, braved
death in her white girlhood.

In the eternal holiday
of heaven's golden weather,
the gentle Lion, the fearless lamb
forever are together.

Sunset [II]

Lay him to rest in full pontificals
upon the purple catafalque of sky.
Stars shall be tapers in the dusk that falls,
greatness must greatly die.

The Vineyard

These wild grapes, few and small and bitter,
are all my vineyard grows—
pull down the press, uproot the vines
in all their futile rows,

sow me this ground with salt, with fire,
no living tendril spare—
"Nay," said a voice beside me then
and I knew the Gardener.

"Nay, in the name of broken reeds,
of dwarfed and stunted trees—
once, wild with thirst, I had welcomed
even sorriest lees. (Drink from even these).

"Plough me once more the vineyard.
Prune me the vines yet again."
'"Yea, Lord," I said in my anguish,
"and tears shall be the rain."

For One Departed

There is no memory of you
in rooms that were your own.
I labor to construct anew
the combination known
so well—to see you in that door,
crossing familiarly this floor.

And yet for all the vacancy,
departure so complete,
a souvenir, whose subtlety
is more than echoing feet,
inhabits, moves, and dominates
this void that it creates.

Strangely I am that absent power
that puts you at my side.
There is not any waking hour
but you confront my pride—
more than the past could count upon
who made so sure that you were gone.

The Traveler

I shall have done with mountains, so I said;
it is outrageous they should steal the sky
as, bulking like a world, they stint the eye
its vested right of vision—country spread
from white sunrise to where the sun sets red.
They are the land's revolt, rebellions' cry
is theirs—"I will not serve"—as proudly high
they hold unbowed their white, imperious head.

I shall go back to humble earth men's feet
tread in the quiet commerce of the corn,
to clover patches bounded by the wood—
Oh, I shall find the flat lands sweet, home sweet,
while paying homage every night and morn
to one far Hill that served, crowned with His Blood!

Unregenerate

I have no patience with the multitude
whose hunger in the desert—not Thine own—
moved Thee to miracle; Thou gavest food
and on the morrow found them bleak as stone.

The woman at the well, impertinent,
a curious talker, argumentative,
had had short shrift of me, had but been sent
upon her way, denied what I might give.

Because, dear Christ, I differ thus from Thee
and by this measure count my sum of fears,
I scourge myself with rods—remember me,
the hard of heart that burns with shame and tears.

Somewhat a Lady Sings

What have I for You, my little One?
(Oh, my breast, my breast!
Exquisite answer of pain to love
by a Baby's lips confessed.)

What have I done to You, O my God?
I have given You birth,
hunger and thirst and houseless head
and a grave in the earth.

(May it not be said in the courts of doom
I bore You to Your death?
How shall the nations bless my name
in the streets of whatever Gath?)

Oh, I have builded You tenderly,
in secret, out of my bone,
to send You walking the winepress,
walking alone, alone!

I have given You fair shoulders
and a brave heart, my Dear,
to carry what coming burdens,
target for what a spear!

Yet what can I do but fold you, now,
adoring, and offer these,
stored with my veins' white wonder,
as witness the prophecies?

The dawn comes gray on Bethlehem,
Jehovah, my own Offspring;
I kiss the blue closed lids of Your eyes,
and I know, and sing.

Distinction

I am the wind that kissed His face,
the air He breathed through me,
next to me only other, came the grace
by which alone lived He.

Before archangels were conceived
or anything began,
Almighty God had me in mind
to be the breath of Man.

God in Man

A shuttered house He occupies
Whose home is wider than the skies.
(On Thabor, all its windows lit,
three men were blinded, seeing it).

He hid His Godhead in some sort,
successfully, by all report.
(Some jars of water once, they say,
rebelled and gave the truth away).

Of Poets who Died in the War

They have had youth, that are so freshly dead,
love and renown, and every gracious sweet
within the reach of questing hands and feet,
and all the hunger of their spirit fed.
They knew not age, but wear its crown instead,
for when life's tale the years at last complete
and dim eyes look out from the chimney seat,
life only lives remembering dear things fled.

In that far time toward the sunset gun,
the veterans shall sit with fancy roving,
winters that must turn backward seeking spring.
But these, these lads who sunk before their sun,
they had their youth, its laughter and its loving,
all, at a moment, that the years may bring.

The Prodigal

Companion me in this dull room,
O Mary's Son!
What have I done,
to wall me with unwindowed gloom?

I know, O satisfying Heart.
And from far lands
with empty hands
I turn within me where Thou art.

Declarations

I cannot pity Him much, little Baby—
so kind are her eyes;
were the inns, after all, such desirable lodging?
In her bosom He lies.
Possibly here there is shortage of bread,
but, see, He is fed.

I would not give one hair of her brow
for all the world's gold.
Turn me the mountain to pearl, what of that?
Her hand I will hold.
Keep the heavens and all unimaginable spheres—
I will treasure her tears.

The Daughter of Jairus

"She is not dead, but sleepeth," so He said
Who giveth His beloved sleep. Taking her hand
He led her back from that other, the living land,
and gave her to the bosoms of the dead.

To Zachary

The mighty messenger who struck you dumb
and sealed your eyes on that announcement day—
reluctant angel knew of things to come
and the shorn part you would be forced to play.
For now eternity but held its breath,
One who had never moved was on the wing,
the Dove that was to light on Nazareth

that wildly wondrous overshadowing.
Soon, too, the Maiden would arise and climb
your hills—Elizabeth in graced accord
carried two secrets, waiting for her time,
John, and that cry, "The Mother of my Lord."
"Magnificat," she sang—the unborn stirred—
and you stood by, and did not hear a word.

Envoy [II]

When Mary's Son was but a Child at play,
a legend tells He fashioned birds of clay
that came to life, and sang, and flew away.

Here is an end of singing, birds of clay,
my songs are lost in sky, their after-way,
nor silence, nor the closing clouds betray.

O Princeling of Thy Father's house of song,
there is no music on our lips for long—
Thou only art Immortal, Holy, Strong!

V. Published Poems [Added 2010]

A Visit to Crown Point

(In Memory of Mr. Burke)

Today I saw your grave,
tended with loving care,
and where the few leaves fell
in the soft September air,
I knelt, as you would have me kneel,
and said a prayer.

I know you felt me there,
though the flowers never stirred,
and to my teeming thoughts
you answered not a word:
there was companionship no less,
and my heart heard.

In the broad fields of heaven—
O, best of all my friends!
You play, a happy child,
a game that never ends,
the game that for your labor here
makes full amends.

Gallant your soul and true
and brave as a man is brave.
Giving, you went your way
and till the last you gave;
sure you are tired, but contented, too,
in your lovely grave.

And I know in some corner of heaven,
the young saints and the old
crowd 'round you every evening
when your good old jokes are told,
and they laugh till they shake the rafters
of God's house of gold.

Notre Dame

How can I tell thee all the ways I love
Thee, Mother, Queen, all fairest things above;
now though our pathways should the long years part,
I ask thee still to keep me in thy heart.

But more than poet's dreams 'twas here I learned
how patriot fires in thee have ever burned,
as history knows, till in my quickening frame
the same sweet passion wakened into flame.

"Haunts of my youth," yes, here did Poetry
first open out her magic scroll to me,
and where the inland ripples leap and dance,
I saw the plunging keels of old romance.

And memory, pausing then to dream awhile,
will see through dimming eyes that still must smile,
and hear across the water's rippling blue,
a shadowy coxswain call a shadowy crew.

Some day returning out of ways more wide,
again the pleasant waters I may walk beside;
seek in old haunts and old accustomed places,
seek—and not find "the old familiar faces."

There is no answer in the fragrant air,
but promise of fulfillment everywhere;
the beauty that each year thou takest new,
out of God's hand proclaims that He is true.

I think of all whose eyes have gazed upon
the beauties thou unveilest to the dawn;
all who a budding springtime here have known—
and wonder where their autumn leaf has blown.

Beside thy lakes, along the shaded ways,
my steps have gone, how many golden days!
I seemed to have a comrade in each tree,
for all were rooted in the heart of thee.

Night comes and sets thy beacon in the skies,
a woman starry-crowned, with starry eyes,
that watch forever with a solace meet
above the glimmering moon beneath her feet.

The jewels of a fallen firmament
gleam on thy snowy lawn with beauty blent,
while underneath, you fancy as you pass,
you hear the murmur of the waiting grass.

For I am minded of that early day
when first their eyes in greeting on thee lay,
Sorin and his brave band, thou wert to them
our lady's mantle, and they kissed its hem.

Howe'er the changing months may come or go,
whatever tones the wind's wild trumpet blow;
thy cheeks are fair, thine eyes with beauty glow,
and lovely, art thou, Lady of the Snow.

Thou art, my Queen, a daughter of the Day;
the lights of heaven about thy temples play,
the full moon whitely crowns thy loveliness,
the sunset lays on thee its last caress.

Let strike thy lofty tower into the blue,
the mossy pathway wind the woodway through;
thou art by wood and walk and hallowed wall
a presence and a power over all.

I only know that on whatever hall
sunlight or moonlight rapturously fall,
that thou, within thy empery of green,
art radiantly beautiful, my Queen.

Is it at the dawning or in star-time dim,
thy towers break the far horizon's rim,
is it in spring or in the summer air?
I only know, my Mother, thou art fair.

God's Poet

For him who smote the harp, the harp is smitten;
for him whose voice was gold, a song we raise,
who greater was and is than all that's written,
said or imagined in his boundless praise.
The man that is the style,
the soul that is the man,
him whole we scan
with vision heaven-loaned a while.
In all his works a poet, he,
chrismed of Christ and Castaly,
whose words enriched the treasure-hoard of time
in lofty thought of prose and rime:
poet, say I, in all his works, 'tis meet
we lay our laurels at the poet's feet.

Poet, the very word is kin of God,
Who made the quiring Cherubim and stars,
the seven chorded harp of light,
alternate chant of day and night;
made lyric every wind and breeze,
toned with tempest or lulling low-strewn bars;
God wrought the surging epic of the seas.
Yea, and the murmuring sod,
all nature, joins into His harmonies.
He gave thee, poet, true and kind,
the poet's eye, the poet's mind;
the noise-disdaining, chastened ear

to catch what few men hear.
He made thy heart a symphony
accord of fit diversity,
wherein the valor of the valiant met
the meek, with eyelids wet.
The lion and the lamb thou wert,
with peace sword-girt.
Thou wert the eagle and the dove,
strong-winged with love.
Thy bounds were Northern fiords and soft South shores of green,
with the glad, strong ocean of thy being flung between.

Thou wert, O poet, seer and sage,
and thou wert more.
He who had writ and folded many a page
in the dim-cloistered rock,
who said, "Let there be light!"
was He who came in weakness dight
and wore
the fool's own robe of white.
Who, dying, 'mid earth's shock,
left thee, when that His head drooped down,
His purple and his crown.

And thou hast worn them all the years—
the poet's royalty of blood and tears—
the poet who is priest and hierarch;
who in the dark,
aloft, away,
learns secrets of the day;
who dwells within the cloud,
above the crowd,
and issues forth a space
with sprit wrung,
Jehovah's lightnings on his face,
and Sinai's thunders on his shaken tongue.

Poet, thy chasuble
became thee well.
Thy singing robes were cloths of pride,
who hadst thy vesture from God's side.

And thou didst weave a strain
where earth and heaven twain
grew one,
till, mighty, lo,
in its full power,
thy song was sudden done!
God made thee mute
as one might hush a lute.
Then art thou silent, so?
Ah, no!
This pregnant hour
no land but owns the valor of thy voice,
while all who hear it wonder and rejoice;
thy silence best of all
is musical.
God, in the interval,
O poet of high grace,
has left His music in thy face
as in a frozen waterfall!
In thy meek amity
and gentle childlikeness
are tones the tempest never woke,
but which are spoke
at dusk-fall in the silver hush of heaven.
for God has made—
Oh, let us tell it loud and free,
yea, even
to every wind on every sea!
God's made a poem of thee—
struck thee, as one might strike a lyre,
whose answer grows a strain
of mingled love and pain
and infinite desire.

Thus, thus is silence fraught
with singing past all thought.
Thou art, O poet, great and strong—
thou art thy song!

The Day of Days

What day, of all the days that run
through mingled shadow and blended sun,
as days have moved since time begun
to make the measured year, shall say
the measure of my life is done,
the battle lost or won—
what day?

When spring is wild, when June is sweet,
when autumn follows rich and fleet;
when winter comes with snow and sleet,
each in its yearly welcomed way,
what day of all the days I greet
shall fold my hands and feet—
what day?

What day, perchance at couch with Night
whose clouded locks are heavy and bright,
in which the stars are gathered white,
shall first behold my moveless clay?
What day shall bring mine eyes the Light
where life is endless quite—
what day?

What day—or do they count the days
whose harps are tuned to timeless praise
of Him who with the white-robed strays,
all wedding-garmented?—shall they
join to their ranks with no amaze
one whom His Blood arrays—
what day?

The Blessed Barren

Sometimes her arm will bend as if to hold
a little head against an eager breast;
her eyes are deep with dream, when she is old
how might her children seek her face for rest.

Her head, it leans so slightly to the side
as if to hear a cricket in the path;
a heart so full of white content could hide
a bruised name within the peace it hath.

But she will go her silver, lonely way
toward heaven, where is neither man nor wife;
there God shall bring her little ones and say:
Their mother grasped, and held, the fire of life.

The Silver Birch

Why should I grieve who deeply love the spring
and all the radiant summer, now the sky
is hidden by grey clouds, and no birds fly
amid the cedar limbs and nest and sing
as late so sweetly? Though bitter north winds bring
death on their icy wings, above them high
glad tidings of the life of them that die
in silence of the shrouded forest ring.

So I can take the season hand in hand,
in face of things the deeper meaning search:
and all the weary journey, patient quite,
regard the loss as gain, with sky and land—
can gather comfort of the silver birch,
whose very widowhood is clothed in white.

Fulfillment

What flail shall take the harvest of the wind,
who lift the halo from the dying star?
Into what prison-house, whose power shall bind
the blue of sky and ocean, trysting far?

The lawless running perfumes of the woods
that meet in mystic ways invisible,
the changing cadences of river moods—
no wizard's wand may circle these with spell.

Only without the confines of their range,
waits One who would not seem to lose them long;
caught up in Him who knows not loss nor change
are seed and starlight, color, perfume, song.

Evening

The heaven, ringed with tossing clouds,
has lately hid its front of flame;
a voice is shepherding the winds
to the wattles whence they came.

On silent fields the blue dusk, thin
and white, above the sunset bars—
where Night's wide temple veil is drawn—
the fire of vestal stars.

Leaves

Ye play with the Wind today,
yielding the kisses he craves—
fools, know ye not next month
he shall hound ye to your graves?

Your mothers, a day ago,
he won as he woos ye now—
hags in their tattered brown,
what count makes he of a vow?

So blows the world away,
the moment, the moment is all;
life is a promise in spring—
how often fulfillment in fall?

Summer's Sacrament

The wheat field bows its heavy head,
the grapes hang from the vine,
and one has offering of bread,
and one a gift of wine.

The word of all—"Consummated"—
cut, thresh, then grind and knead;
and One from Bosra He shall tread
the grapes that yearn to bleed.

Twilight

In carmine cloak the gipsy Day
knocked at Eve's monastery bars;
now comes he, novice cowled in gray,
to light the candles of the stars.

Treasures

Old things and new are His: this green,
gay garment of the Maiden Spring,
is it some new, wide, wondrous thing,
or robe that Eden's fields have seen?

The Underground Trolley

In starless shadow and alone,
I labor, still as stone.
Through me, the lightning's fatal darts
make live a million hearts.

A tireless-throbbing nerve of fire,
I yoke the dock and spire.
To dusty streets green hills I chain
where dim eyes laugh again.

And I have power, though mute of voice,
to make dull ears rejoice—
a thousand ripples, lapping warm,
call in my quivering arm.

I lead the cramped and time-worn heart
to solitudes apart—
I am to every satyr man
the timeless pipes of Pan.

The Poets

This one out of his heart made song,
and this one out of his brain:
delicate, deft, with a quaint refrain,
it entered the fancy and lingered long,
to echo but dim in the day of pain.

But he who forged the song in his heart
bared the soul of the world in his tune.
Men lightly listened, and passed, but the rune
came back to them when they wept apart
in the winter's sorrow that trod down June.

The poets met: the singer said,
"Ah, if I could but touch the heart."
And the seer sighed, "In contempt I smart
till the soul of the world with grief has bled."
And sorrowing still they moved apart.

The fathomless word and the airy rhyme
both from the heart's deep knowledge grow,
out of the heart's own fret they flow,
and the poet will grieve till the end of time—
that his song is thence he will never know.

The Poet's Providence

He that hath watched the sparrow's wing
creation long,
as well hath ear for a little thing,
even my song.

He that hath loomed the bridal snow
of the lily's dress,
will clothe my poorer heart, I know,
with light no less.

Wheat Fields

Not less than Cana's wave
that leaped to wine
at the sudden sign
Thy Filial spirit gave;

these at Thy timed command
shed the gold wheat
that turns out Meat
within Thy creature's hand.

The Immaculate Conception

When thou wert born the stars sang in their spheres,
as round and round they swung in endless space,
happy that all the waiting of long years
was o'er—one heart was born solely of grace;
and on the gray of old Judea's hills
a joy fell, holy as an angel's prayer—
a peace, full of the rapturous joy which fills
our hearts today, made soft the throbbing air.
Archangels wrought for thee a lullaby;
thou, queen of heaven, crowned before thy birth,
wert named Immaculate before the sky
held sun or stars to rift the night of earth.
He ordered so, thine uncreated Child,
born of thee, Mother, Maiden undefiled.

St. John of the Apocalypse

His thoughtful eyes bent on the weary waste
of sea that holds bleak Patmos captive-bound,
his dull ears heeded not the lapping sound
of waves that, broken, kiss the beach and haste
away. His spirit dreamed, a sweet foretaste
of that great dream to come. His mantle round
about him lay unloosed; his soft hair, crowned
with flame, fell on a brow as new snow chaste.

When, lo! a trumpet-voice behind him spoke,
shaking the air with its empowered breath.
He turned—the light of God upon him broke
in ocean floods of might. Like one in death,
he fell upon the sands in sleep serene—
soul-lifted to that place "eye hath not seen."

Exiled Nuns

A little house is all they ask,
a garden with a plot of flowers,
where they may ply their daily task,
giving to God the simple hours.

The morrow comes, the morrow goes;
each day the selfsame work and prayers—
under the shrouding veil, who knows
the silent suffering that is theirs?

A quiet broods within their wall—
it is the quiet of the tomb.
No novice comes to the Master's call,
none comes to take the empty room

of her they laid away last year
under this alien grass and dew—
ah, were not autumn hopeless drear
if 'neath old leaves slept not the new?

But these, their name will drop away—
oh, bitter cup the exile sips!
Yet martyr-like they wait the day
with patient heart and prayerful lips.

These lilies of the fields of France,
rich roses of the Breton sod—
no word of mine can e'er enhance
the fragrance of their life for God.

A Friend

Unbidden tears stood in his eyes unshed
as soft the parting words to me he said;
he slowly turned away,
and passed forever from my strained sight
into the dusk, prelude of coming night
and winding-sheet of day.
How sad on winter's air the sound of passing bell!
Yet heavier hung my soul
beneath its weight of grief than ever funeral toll
upon a sin-swept heart in wakening terror fell.

The Stranger Hills

The stranger hills are blue, friend,
and fair fields lie between,
and friends are here that are true, friend,
but yet is the thought of you
full first in my heart, and the fields we knew,
and the hills of the life that has been.

The west is dim, yet the sun, friend,
has left stars piling there
to shape my dreaming of one, friend;
and an evening when all was done,
we looked in the dusk on our long day run,
with a peace that was half despair.

For then 'neath the garnet skies, friend,
in the gray of the twilight lands,
we silenced the last good-byes, friend,
and blunted the edge of a thousand sighs;
but deep called to deep in the parting eyes—
oh, the treason of lingering hands!

Encompassed

"In Whom we live and move and are."

The least, most instant thoughts I think
win to Thy mind;
Thou art most kind.

My feet with weariness may sink—
ere I can cry
lo, Thou art by.

Yea, when upon the awful brink
of death I stand
I hold Thy hand.

Only for this aghast I shrink
at deeps of hell,
"God lost," they spell.

And when of utter bliss I drink,
what shall it be
but Thee, but Thee.

Fortitudo et Pax: The Bishop and His See

The Phantasy in Verse—In honor of the Rt. Rev. Joseph Sarsfield Glass, D.D.,
   Bishop of Salt Lake. Written for the Holy Cross Sisters, St. Mary's Academy,
   Salt Lake.

The Spirit of Salt Lake speaks:
I am the Lady of the Lake, behold
the soundless waters of my inland sea,
the crusted scud of salt, the lacy foam
that folds me round in ancient mystery.
I am the daughter of that silent time
when foot of man or beast upon the plain
challenged the empire of my sweeping tide.
Of old I saw the bearded mountains rise.
I gave the glaciers of the past Good Night.
I cannot count how many wandering stars
are sunken in my heart, and every day
I sail the red Armada of the sun.
For I am very old and very young,
ages as days go by, and I abide.

Chorus of Waves:
For she is very old and very young,
ages as days go by, and she abides.

The Spirit of Salt Lake:
My days are sacred by a double token,
by nature's claim, and by a right divine:
and though one fail, though all my salty tide
the thirsting centuries at length consume,
still shall I stand immortal and a queen.
For I am wedded to a deathless lord
and share his beauteous immortality.

Chorus of Waves:
For she is wedded to a deathless lord
and shares his beauteous immortality.

The Spirit of Salt Lake:
There was a bark, ye know the story well,
wherein sat fishers of an inland sea
or mended nets beside it on the sand,
until one day Genesareth's white foam
rushed o'er the rocks to fall upon the feet
of Him who walked the world that He had made:
rushed in a sweet embrace of flood and foam
to kiss His feet, a sinless Magdalen.

Chorus of Waves:
Rushed in a sweet embrace of flood and foam,
to kiss His feet, a sinless Magdalen.

The Spirit of Salt Lake:
The fishers mending nets looked up and heard
creative bidding: for the Voice that bade
the primal waters and the land divide
now made the whole broad earth a mystic sea
for Peter's bark to sail, and Peter's nets
went gathering fishes of the souls of men.

Chorus of Waves:
Now made the whole broad earth a mystic sea
for Peter's bark to sail, and Peter's nets
went gathering fishes of the souls of men.

The Spirit of Salt Lake:
And Peter's keel so found my salty sea.
His net my bosom dragged: I gave him forth
souls and unnumbered to his trusty care
who first was Bishop of this hallowed seat
and late has won the crown his work was worth.

Chorus of Waves:
Who first was Bishop of this hallowed seat
and late has won the crown his work was worth.

The Spirit of Salt Lake:
And lo! another pilot comes, another prince,
a newer shepherd of a newer day—
I bid him welcome here with all my tide.
I await his blessing and acclaim his power.
Witness his wedding to his spousal sea.

Chorus of Waves:
We await his blessing and acclaim his power.
Witness his wedding to his spousal see.

(Enter the Bishop's Ring)

The Gold Band Speaks:
We are that ring of gold
whereby, of old,
Venetian lords, for so the legends run,
held gleaming in the sun,
then cast into the sea,
assuming sovereignty
over the city, bosomed on that tide,
and Venice took as bride.
We are that gold the New Jerusalem
wears, lit with many a gem,
pure gold without alloy,
symbol of heaven's joy.

The Amethyst Speaks:
An amethyst are we,
blue as the deep, still sea.
mined in the caves of night
to flash the morning's light
blue as the incense smoke,
blue as our Lady's cloak;
in night's blue mystery,
a star of constancy.

The Spirit of Salt Lake:
O Band of Gold, O Stone of Blue,
united be in marriage true.
Ye Waves and Waters, rise and sing,
a Bishop's ring, a Bishop's ring!

Chorus of Waves:
Into our waters flash and fling
the Bishop's ring, the Bishop's ring!

The Spirit of Salt Lake:
Lo, it is done, and Peace and Strength,
upon the Waters walk at length.

All:
Courage and peace his days enfold
who wears our jeweled band of gold.
Let peace be in thy strength
and sweeten all thy powers.
Let peace be in thy strength,
and abundance in thy towers.

On Founder's Day

This is the tree whose root he set
that bitter spring in stubborn soil:
God's sunny grace and man's hard toil
have reared it thus, nor fail it yet.

Against all seasons grew its girth,
by storm unshook, by drought unshrunk,
a naked, scarred but living trunk
fire left it once—still firm in earth.

A tree of many branches now
it towers among time's mighty ones,
the mothering home of many sons,
the fruit of Sorin's triple vow.

I saw a cedar hacked and thrown
upon the common wood-pile—red
was all its core, as if some fled
fair sunset to its heart had flown.

Not so thy power shall depart,
O Notre Dame, but there shall be
the things that grace eternity
stored golden in thy wide, warm heart.

And when some distant dawn shall see
thy splendor gone, when worlds are dead
and all the feet of time have fled,
God's mind shall keep thy memory.

Twilight [II]

No longer at the western wall contends
the valiant sun with leaguering clouds at bay,
but darkness like a silent rain descends
upon the smoldering ruins of the day.

A Child Prays for Me

There are great wings about her
to guard against all harms:
her father's angel—he is dead—
her own, and her mother's arms.

Within that sanctitude she moves
with look and movement bright;
the flutter of those pinions leave
her cheek now red, now white.

Within the garden of her mind
the whitest lilies grow—
the little thoughts that through her speech
in simple fragrance flow.

It was her thought that day by day
one thought should spring for me,
and she should lay it in God's hand
for my felicity.

And so she takes her morning way—
I seem to see her there—
unto His throne, with heaven's light
bathing her childish hair.

Around her are those saints whose robes
had never lost their white,
and One whose mantle has the hue
with which her eyes are bright.

She lays the lily in God's hand—
why should she feel afraid?
Only the exiled one whose name
she breathes is sore dismayed.

She does not know the deep unworth,
the need, the gloom, the fears—
he only knows whose promised hand
shall wipe away all tears.

He only knows who was a Child
and born of Maid most fair,
Who bides within her latticed heart,
the Gardener of her prayer.

So all my days and all my nights
her prayers are in God's hand—
No wonder that, her clasp in mine,
I walk a holy land.

Village Churches

God help you, little churches,
that were the help of God,
a broken-hearted host that War
shattered, and spurned, and trod—
you are the saddest ruins left
above the saddest sod!

A hundred years, a thousand,
you were the holy place,
an ocean and a river
of the white tides of grace
now only stones and mortar
and in the dust, your face.

You were the happy prison
that Love's great Captive chose
to have among His children

His house and His repose,
where all the saints like lilies
bloomed round the Mystic Rose.

O sundered bars, O broken cage,
O God that was your Bird,
no more within His secret bower
the Dove's low voice is heard,
the rain falls through your open roof
and you are all unstirred.

O lonely little villages
where never God comes by,
no nearer than the heavens,
the far and fearful sky—
Who used to dwell within you,
the Apple of your Eye.

I speak not of cathedrals
whose ruin robs the arts,
but little village churches
and broken village hearts
where living faith and love abide
though hope almost departs.

Almost, but they are minded
of deeper than this gloom,
the age-long hours of anguish
and the dead Bridegroom,
and all in a sunny morning
an invincible tomb.

Dear Christ, these little churches,
You were their only pride,
I crawl into their ruins
as into Your wounded side,
and know that in the Church, Lord,
You evermore abide.

VI. Manuscripts [Added 2010]

For Charles Phillips, His Father

I see him standing in the uncleared wood,
himself an oak, as hardy and austere,
without reproach among his own, or fear,
he took the virgin ways of solitude
and looking in that wildness called it good.
Blazing the trail, this more than pioneer
saw lives to be both innocent and dear,
and great with destinies he understood.

So, for your sake and others that should pass
he squared the logs for God's house in the North
where winter's heel is hard on fields and brooks;
and, purposeful, when he had housed the Mass,
he reared one calf whose skin should furnish forth—
ah, faith!—a binding for the Book of Books.

The Visitation

Carmel against the distant west
stood blue as she arose
with the wild secret in her breast—
fired by a fire of snows—
and set her footsteps to the south,
Magnificat stirring in her mouth.

Before she came to Hebron town
five suns of spring had set,
and there was dust upon her gown,
with dew her hair was wet:

but rivers sweeping to the sea
were not so strong and pure as she.

The bitter winds of March were out,
that touched her cheek to tears,
the white moon compassed her about,
alone with her white fears—
this little flower of Jesse's rod
whose breast was burgeoning with God.

Companioned, to her cousin's door
she came on love's light feet,
her shadow fell across the floor;
and dawn flames not so fleet
as joy broke in Elizabeth,
and loyalty that leaps to death.

They kissed and stroked each other's face,
and laughed a little, and cried;
and then the traveler, full of grace,
sang, or her heart had died.
Magnificat—O listening womb!—
Anima mea Dominum.

Kostka

When Stanislaus, whose sires with heart of steel
stood between Europe and the Saracen
a thousand years, would leave those fighting men
and join another host whose quickened zeal
engaged a fiercer foe, an iron heel
stamped at him: "What, a Prince of Poland—when
had any Kostka fled to the soutane,
buried his arms, his name!" In vain, appeal
to that proud race. Yet only by his weakness
we know their power, and but for his bright shame,
but for the memory of his terrible meekness,
their valor were forgotten, and their name.
While all his sweetness, like a crystal glass,
shows us the lady that his mother was.

Hymn of Light

I

A light is dawning in the eastern sea,
the waters are aware, and all the tide
with lifted lips pants toward the breaking day.
Heaven is tremulous with birth, and Night,
lain on the silver shallop of the moon,
like some old king with higher throne than power,
sails the pale wide circumference of the west,
while down the path of light that darkens him
have fled in rout his blackened fleet of stars.
It is the sunrise of an early spring when float
the palest splendors over earth and sky,
the sky a blossom on the leaf of earth
whose fruitage is a June of singing larks.
Cloud-daisies hang above the branching sea
that is their trunk and root; invisible
from spumy soil through grain of sunlight mounts
the sap that flowers the sky—who sail the sea
are dryads of an elemental wood.
Where are the depths in ocean or in earth
that do not answer on a rising day
adsum unto the light's conspiracy.
Death, temporal tenant of the realms of life,
shakes at the general muster; the robin's note
rings like a bell, "I know, I know"; laughing
the winds take up the echo and repeat
"I know"; grasses bend over sighing, "Yes,"
the moving brooklet dimples with assent,
old Earth is ready full to speak for those—
mammoth and man, stone, water, tree and fire
housed in her heart; they too but wait the hour,
and all the bones of ocean ask "How long?"

Word of Light

I am He, Son of the Father, Sun,
Orient, Star of the Morn, in One.

151

Others He made,
Me He begot;
them he arrayed,
Me He did not
in web of the colors of sunset unfurled:
all they in Me
conjoined be,
rays that array all the pride of the world,
yet am I colorless quite,
naked and white.
On Me who gaze
ne'er again raise
eyes from the sod,
blinded by God.
Others He made,
Me He begot.
Them He arrayed,
Me He did not.
So am I Light,
naked and white.

II Sword of Light

Yet shall He reach His own. Pound on, pound on,
ye hammers beating blood and bones to gold,
ye grinding wheels that from a maiden's hands
weave silken shadows for the house of shame;
let fall the cutting smoke on eyes that yet
have never drunk the twilight nor have seen
the rose of dawn grow golden at the heart.
In this stern time, not for the jungle I,
nor those old Northern woods, the home of Night,
bespeak the blessing of an open day.
But through the world's black mockery of life
that towers upon the wreck of human souls,
juttied and pinnacled on blasted souls,
city and town, the factory and the store,
that starve, bleed, blacken, curse and cheapen men,
through these I call the sundering sword of Light

152

avenging and arighting: then shall ring
the thunder notes of justice in the day,
dawn lay an even kiss on all mankind,
and evening come, and night grow sweet with stars.
For God is Light,
His is the right,
and though awhile He seem to sleep,
His hands the lightnings keep,
and He the Day.
Aloft, away,
I see them in a golden weather,
on dewey hills, inherited of Light,
these poor others, not these, shall know that nether
fires are not bright.

Reflections on My Mother's State in Heaven

Granting His presence, you are fully happy
because His Mother will be somewhere near
and reaching out to touch her if some misgiving
conceivably should rise, would end your fear.
And add to this the circumstance of light,
your only terror here was dread of night.
There would be, too, this circumstance to mark—
light, light for your life-long terror of the dark.

Only a fraction of Omnipotence—
which nonetheless implies the awful whole—
would quite suffice to make and minister
the peace that is the heaven of your soul.
Here, after winter, when the flowers awake,
you were not one who would interrogate.

No visitor, not one, for stir or sound
you kept with sheltered care a sturdy flame.
Going to Mass as needs be, when you went
you were as sweet as when from Mass you came.
The whole assumption of your quiet art
of living was that God was in your heart.

Loving intensely with a quiet fury,
there was some bargain, something understood.
One fierce demand, you made, I think, of heaven,
some right you based upon your innocent blood.
It would concern the children of your womb.
Your gray eyes prayed and challenged God for whom.

Biding in peace with heaven's substitute,
whatever that may be—within your fingers—
even your paradise must know the beads—
your confident soul in Mary's circle lingers
knowing that we shall come at last to you
for all that I have said of you is true.

The Passion

The serpent, Mary, turns on thee,
although beneath thy heel he smarts,
since on thyself no power has he,
and fangs thee in thy Heart of Hearts.

The Death Angel Speaks at Heaven's Gate

(for Sergeant Joyce Kilmer, killed in action, July 30, 1918)

Saint Michael, Prince of Angels and Captain of the charge
that filled the void of Hell with broken wings,
a sergeant I bring you, a soldier of the line,
the battle line, the line of saints, the ancient line that sings.

Lance-hurler of the heaven wars, Michael of the sword,
admit him to your ranks and give command,
what bid you of valor, of virtue, of beauty—
he has the level eyes that understand.

A sergeant I bring you, of Christ's wars a veteran,
a singer whom David may entrust with his song—
I saw him, I loved him, I took him, receive him,

Saint Michael, your sergeant and his clean heart strong.

Vita

Our life is His Whose life as man
in her unsullied breast began.
The streams that flow down any mountain
she is their fountainhead and fountain.

Dulcedo

A bitter taste was left by Eve
in life's own love until reprieve
we earned by her whose winsomeness
eternal God must needs confess.

Spes

Despair and doubt she put to flight
who bore our Savior in the night.
Mother of Him, our Queen of grace,
perpetual morning in her face!

In All His Glory

There are beyond the power of kings
the simple flower things.
Let Solomon surround the sea,
a rose will beggar argosies.
His mines may strip the rib of earth
of gold, but who the lily's girth?
Who fired the sun has seen to it
that sunflowers in the lane be lit.
Who thought archangels set the tall
hollyhocks by the garden wall.

He is beforehand all the way—
let the small kings have their day.

The King

It was a crowned head that drooped
at the last breath
drawn when life stooped
to the low door of death.
But it was not the crown
bowed His head down.

Hallow and light that wreath
although a fire of pain
burns in it—underneath
His brow was touched in vain.
He loved the thorns He wore,
and that low-linteled door.

Stoop, stoop, my heart, the King
is lowly laid:
drink of that cup, the thing
of which you are afraid—
pain, shame, reproaches—these
are crowns and royalties.

New Saints for Old

Infinite God, whose loveliness
no one completely compasses—
the great procession yet shall wend
its way along until time's end,
of those who show some single trace
of that which is Thy perfect grace.

Agnes that was shall be again,
a hundred Daniels walk the den;
another Lawrence laid in fire

shall twit his torturers like his sire,
and fair Caecilias, throng on throng,
shall rifle heaven of its song.

Adventurers like him who trod
the Indies and Japan for God
shall take their wings and travel far
beyond the palest challenging star—
his lips shall hive what golden bees
who preaches to the Pleiades!

Though lamps burn low to Anthony,
and Christopher be lost at sea,
the poor shall have their dole of bread
and travelers be safely led.
Some other Rita shall dispense
impossible favors, ages hence.

O ever ancient, ever new
Beauty, one, infinite and true,
no one of us can gauge, can guess
the limits of Thy loveliness
in whom are lost both near and far,
wave beyond wave, star beyond star.

[Cancelled stanza #4 of "New Saints for Old"]
Like petals dropping from the rose
as yesteryear and all its snows
find in the fleeting flowers or grass
these that we know today may pass—
The Little Flower may fade and die
and Lourdes may weep a spring gone dry.

[Another cancelled stanza #4 of "New Saints for Old"]
No matter. Lo! an avalanche
where all was but a fount in France—
shall slip some Himalayan height
and Mary clad in snows and light
shall stand there smiling pure and sweet
with Bernadette kneeling at her feet.
[while all the world climbs to her feet.]

157

[Cancelled stanza #6 of "New Saints for Old"]
The forty martyrs of Sebaste
a myriad martyrs at the last—
from Russian steppes, from Labrador
who knows what hidden links may pour,
preeminence from pole to pole
Christ's holy image in their soul.

The Bees

All summer time they packed their cold
cells in the gathered sweetness, hived
the sun, against these nights
when yellow lights
of wax contrived
return
the sum of stolen gold
as candles burn.

Ad Dexterem

I have been looking to Thy right hand from my youth:
there sitteth Christ
and there, folded and safe and sweet, the just
shall gather quietly that day of days
when the last words that He shall ever speak shall have been spoken—
"Come, ye blessed"
and—"Depart."
Love's rendezvous, hope's triumph, faith's reward,
Right Hand of God!
A noonday shade, light in the dark, O Hand of Peace!
Warm-clasping comforter and guide,
O powerful Hand,
Signal that opens the everlasting doors of pearl,
lay on me now Thy blessing,
lay Thy rod!

Consummation

Prophets and kings have desired to see what I have seen—
straw, and a breathing Child?
Moses, Melchisedech, David, to look on the Nazarene—
blood, and a crowd grown wild?
Yes, and of all the holy queens there is not one holy queen
but had kissed His face, defiled.

Mothers are Martyrs

Before the seven swords were drawn
that pierced your heart, there, still and dim,
long months before that Christmas dawn,
you gave your blood for Him.

Christ in the Eucharist

He lives next door to me,
I meet Him every day,
we talk familiarly,
He would have it that way.

This much you may record,
if record there should be,
he lived with the Lord
as His contemporary.

VII. Fragments [Added 2010]

Memories of Notre Dame

Days gone by, golden sky,
autumns and marching men:
drums and cheers, happy years,
hark! how they march again.

Pledges of bravery and tenderness
proudly our loyal loves profess—
O Gold and Blue! there is no one like you,
Notre Dame, Notre Dame.

[Skyscrapers are but streets on end]

Skyscrapers are but streets on end
in the modern city's plan,
behind their shining windows works
the harmless highwayman.

[The pool of poetry is calm]

The pool of poetry is calm
under blue summer skies,
as one by one upon its breast
I cast my stock of flies—
like silver trout the fancies fly
beneath, but will not rise.

Humor

When it comes to finest drollery
I vote for your Tom-foolery,
and as for choicest raillery
there's nothing like Tom-Dailying.

[Merry Christmas to you]

Merry Christmas to you, Brother Matthias,
you never yet have failed to buy us
greeting cards that are sure to please—
issued by the Bengalese.
God bless your house, your barn, your dairy,
yourself and your vocabulary!

[I should not care to see just now]

I should not care to see just now
a bud break out on any bough
nor give much credit in the wood
to any robin's hardihood.

I do not think that I was meant
to go about for my content,
the better system seems to be
to stay at home till come to me
little by little spring's advances.

[High hills, the Alps, and after that the sun]

High hills, the Alps, and after that the sun
that leaves his golden fire along the snow—
the eye gives praise as the eagles go
to win those dizzy peaks the day has won
and died in winning: now that day is done

the stars break into play with silken flow
as Tuscan artists lead, then wait to show
about the hour of saints their courses run.

This is that Italy that Dante bore,
that Shakespeare dreamed of, Browning sang, and Keats
took to his breast, as Shelley took its flood.
Now we are come in harrowing of war,
our living deed, their dreaming tale complete
in the immortal scripture of our blood.

[Cancelled lines 13, 14 for "High hills"]
The dreaming past the shining present meets—
beauty and freedom dying in our blood.

[Another set of cancelled lines 13, 14 for "High hills"]
Piety and beauty down from their high seat
to read the immortal scripture of our blood.

After Communion

I will go to the Holy Land which is my soul [heart],
a pilgrimage of grace, not to the tomb
where He was laid, dead in His winding sheet,
but where He lives and treads my spirit's doom.

Non horruisti uturo Virginis

This is that nuptial chamber long ago
foreshadowed where the brow of Eve
was lifted to the first man's lips.
Divine, the Bridegroom cometh, my God,
and not, poor race, the Bride.

[Now while we wait the ivory]

Now while we wait the ivory
that among towers of clouds withhold,
O Lady, every common tree
gleams like a house of gold.

And daily as the westering sun
goes goldenly to his repose
our rapturous vision rests upon
a man, Thou regal, Mystic Rose.

Far from us here the sea, whose star
Thou art, O gracious Queen,
rolls tumbling all its tides along
majestic, solemn, green.

[I can conceive Thérèse will be forgotten]

I can conceive Thérèse will be forgotten
and Lourdes become a mere remembered name,
so far extend those ages misbegotten
and infinite the fire that feeds their flame.

Yes, like a rose that feels the kiss of summer
unseal its beauty, so the fair may fade
with gradual approach since fair newcomer
may take the crown in other hours now laid.

But I am certain out of Labrador
or some Malayan coast by some lost sea
another flower shall spring and then shall pour

waters of suave immaculate purity.
Today this fountain and this flower are bright—
who shall set limits to the Infinite?

Christ to the Soul

When you have nothing left to give but
cold hands and lips whose early bloom is fled,
should it surprise you in that graying twilight
to find My love is dead?

Will you remember there in early morning,
a June of beauty lit the earth and skies,
I laid a Heart before you for the scorning
of proud averted eyes.

Magnificent, it was not yours the losing!
And time's revenge is one I can but rue,
and this reward which is not of My choosing—
that now I pity you.

The Child

O Helplessness that art Eternal Power,
O silent-seeming Voice of all that sings,
crowded and crushed, compacted in an hour,
Eternal, Source and Ending of all things!

This is inevitable. Assume the role
of Infant, and maintain Thy native awe,
what human wilds of flesh, a human soul
and flash from infant eyes Eternal Law?

Ah, no! Thy wisdom were at fault in this
if one bruised reed of all our stricken band
could not declare Thee Brother, bend and kiss
with kindred lips Thy helpless human hand.

VIII. Dubia [Added 2010]

A Boy

I met him in a crowded train,
a boy who with the sun and rain
all summer in the fields had roamed:
brown cheeks he had, the hair wind-combed,
eyes ripe with dream as sheaves with grain.

We were strange fellows, he and I;
my ready word with him came shy.
His speech went rippling like a song,
and all the while we laughed along
I heard the years go groaning by.

How should I know what things we said:
I know the sun sunk early red,
over low fallows in the Jersey sky;
there was a hurried, bright good-bye,
and a thoughtful hour of joy was dead.

And who am I, with little grace,
that seek a memory to trace
of a vanished boy? Know I am one
treading the flints of life alone,
who wait to see one perfect Face.

Now from my way borne darkly far,
now walking where the white blooms are,
still with a roving, eager heart:
clasping at shadows for my part
yet hungry-hopeful of the Star.

The Crucifix

This is that bush the prophet saw
wherein revealed the Maker stood,
and lo, the bloom that on it grows—
red roses of the falling Blood.

To Francis Thompson

Whatever way his footsteps trod
he saw the burning thoughts of God,
for him there swept from star to tree
a constant Benedicite—
Te Deum, choired the sea.
He saw upon the nest
red Credo of the robin's breast.
The winds in maddest rout
yet Gloria shout.
Rabboni, tremblingly
sang Earth as loosed her hair
fell flowing on Day's red feet in the west.
Lo there, and mostly there
he saw the Vision blest,
o'erbrimming sign of Sunset's falling blood.
The weeping Magdalen.
Now He is gone, and Night,
in death's despite,
against His tomb the stone of darkness rolls,
until He come again,
beating with power upon Time's eastward bars.
Till then, till then,
His pledge of dawn, the Eucharist of stars.

Rain

I am an exile in the cloud,
nor am I native of the earth;
my only garment is a shroud
of mist, my death is but rebirth.

Friendship

Were I a waiting seraph at His seat
and drew therefrom the fadeless ecstasy,

I'd leave that joy and glory at His feet
to come a guardian spirit unto thee.

Battle

There is red battle in the west—
until the fight is won
would that some Moses' lifted arms
might aid the falling sun.

Paganism

In plumage of her stars,
night swept the ancient skies
till at their orient bars
the Sun, Christ, should arise.

Autumn's Sacrament

Ye knights that seek the wide world o'er
and in your emprise nobly fail,
by autumn's vineyards pass no more—
her winepress is the Holy Grail.

Possession

They have the books who hold the keys
of sealed rooms apart—
not theirs the books, but mine who keep
their words within my heart.

The Changeling

I have nursed the baby Song
at my breast,
days and nights, a vigil long,
without rest.

For I feared to lift mine eyes
from his face,
lest the nursling of the skies
flee apace.

Thus it was in days apart
that he fled,
leaving something on my heart
old and dead.

The Celibate

I meet them everywhere I go—
children: they make my gray life glow
with bright return of foresworn dreams,
as wage they now, though scarce it seems,
most dire assault my heart can know.

I never count the veteran smiles
of other lips as leaguring wiles,
nor fear their charge of serried arms,
nor dread in words a lure of harms
save those set thoughtless in the child's.

So keeps their talk mine armor bright,
their pure eyes panoply my sight;
else would their sweet, unplanned surprises
quite vanquish me; their vision rises
and sentinels my sleeping night.

Life [II]

Like flakes will fall the years that now
hang buds of Maytime on the brow.
Life is a wind that blows all ways—
of youth and age the stay art Thou.

Consummated

What marriage this
with gall-lipped kiss
on thorny pillowed bed
consummated?

It was a tomb,
the sterile womb
of man, till in it poured
His life up-stored.

'Twas curtained red
with Blood the bed
of that most fruitful Cross
where lost was loss.

Who die and bleed
a long-lived seed
may see: Life bowed His head
and left Death dead.

Ave Crux

O mystic tree whose sap
doth outward go,
and, to our fruitful hap,
a downward flow.

Longinus

A loud knock he gave
when sharp the spear he drave,
and we with grinding heel
followed that opening steel.
Than heaven's door less low,
the proud unstooping go;
to some that swings not wide
who here may pass Thy side.

Dowry

I haven't a roof or a cot, Neil,
no, nor a single sod:
my Paisley shawl is thin
and my feet are meanly shod,
but my heart is fresh as the day, Neil,
dropped from the hand of God.

I haven't the way o' the world, Neil,
lady's manner and look.
Hardly a line I can write
and I spell out the Mass in my book,
but my thoughts are white as the Bread, Neil,
that we both at the altar took.

I haven't traveled at all, Neil,
though I have crossed the foam,
for the soul o' me always has been

on the blue far hills o' home.
A Donegal girl o' your town, Neil,
into your house, I come.

And you, the man o' my heart, Neil,
will find me ever so
as I am on this May morn
when the winds of our weddin' blow:
I bring you the field o' my life, Neil,
itself with your own life sow.

The Poet's Winter

All his heart is warm beneath its snow,
for spring is there embosomed: yet shall blow
warm winds upon his silent winter, so
the rills of melody shall break and flow.

Experience

Old Honor and young Love
fell out as they trudged along,
for Honor was wroth that Love
left him for a bird's brief song.

(She was young: with eager heart
Love from the path would stray
to pick some dripping bloom
that mocked the dusty way.)

They parted: Honor strode
with stern sorrow on—
Love took the open fields
swift-footed as the dawn.

She flitted, like a moth,
from scent to scent all day,
till twilight closed the flowers
and stole their tints away.

When night came, starless, vast,
and great dew shook down,
in charmless fields Love wept,
yet feared grave Honor's frown.

(Old Honor, wise of heart,
had waited up the way
to take her to his heart
at the white-dawned day.)

She came, with dew-wet robe;
on her face a shadow lay
of pain, and a light of peace:
she said, "Thou are the way."

The Pilgrim

On western ways the Day droops all undone—
unreached the shrine whereto his feet aspire;
yea, but the temple's God he finds, the Sun,
laid on his breast, viaticum of fire.

O Jesus, by the Blood that Flowed

O Jesus, by the Blood that flowed
from those dear Hands of Thine
when cruel nails were driven through
by sinful hands of mine,
forgive the crimes of all today
who raised their hands to sin
and let those Bleeding Wounds of Thine
a pardon for them, win.

O Jesus, by the Blood that flowed
from Thy dear Sacred Head,
when malice wove Thy Crown of Thorns
and mocked Thy circlet red,

forgive the thoughts of those who sinned
against Thy law today
and let Thy bleeding thorn-pierced Brow
a pardon for them, pray.

O Jesus, by the Tears that flowed
from those sweet Eyes of Thine,
when brutal hands uplifted were
to strike those Eyes Divine,
forgive the eyes that sinned today
that dare not look on Thee,
let Tears of Thine plead for them, Lord,
that they, Thy Light, may see.

Christ in the Trenches

I dreamed I saw the Master—that He came
along the F Trench to Varago Sap
and so, by K 14, to Breda Gap.
He stood so straight—although His feet were lame—
it seemed the trench-top hardly hid His cap.

"Oh, Sir, take cover when You pass this way,
the Hun shoots well—a man must guard his head—"
and then I saw His brow was streaming red
and in each hand a pitiful great hole—
hardly there was a place He had not bled.

"Laddie, this cheek has felt the shame anew,
this temple, torn by every falling spire,
they crucified afresh on No-man's wire,
yet high my head is, for the Souls of you
rise in a new-found glory—cleansed by fire."

I dreamed I saw the Master—then I waked
and both my cheeks were wet, as wet with dew
and I stood up, and all the trench seemed new
and there was something in my throat that ached—
but something in my breast beat strong and true.

IX. Advice to the Poets

Dear Algernon:

Your mother mentions in a recent letter that you are writing verse and getting some of it published in the college magazines. I judge from the casualness of your mother's remark that she is all but consumed with pride— the pride that is called pardonable—over your achievement. And that is all right. Perhaps our family can support another poet, even a poet in each generation. Do not think I am writing to point out the error of your ways or the pitfalls that lie in wait for you, or to upbraid you for an undutiful nephew in not letting me see what you have been doing. Rather, as a brand not quite snatched from the burning myself—"an old, cold ash pile" do I hear you say?—I am keen about the fire itself. If you will allow me just this one little fling, let me say I am interested in the integrity of the art of poetry itself.

Once, when I was about your age and had far less sense than you, I wrote to a poet asking him if he would criticize my work. Not to make things worse than they are, nor to let them be as badly as they appear, I must say, in justice to the gosling I was, that the idea upon which I acted was not mine. No, a professor, who should have known better, instigated the affair. The cranky old poet wrote me, on one of those standard, one-cent, yellow postal—not post—cards as follows:

> Living in a house of glass,
> I cast no stones at those who pass.

I think you can guess who this poet was. While the idea was my professor's, the snub was all mine. Yet it has done me no good. Not indeed that I ever again acted upon such advice, but, I mean, the poet's example has done me no good. All my life I have been giving advice: true, it is always advice sought, even demanded, by poets of various degree. As you know, some several hundreds of student-poets like yourself have passed their work to me. I have been a reader of thousands of manuscript poems submitted for print. Accordingly, when I hear that you are turning out stanzas I can't help being interested, nor can I help expressing my interest in the form of advice.

I think I know pretty well what you will write about first and how you will write. The poetry of the young is always old. No doubt this is to be expected. The young read the "models," as they are called, and seem to feel that they have to write accordingly. Unconsciously they assume that certain words and certain ranges of ideas are required for poetry, and they give us, almost with the enthusiasm of discoverers, the old, worn-out themes, in the old, worn-out phrases. Let me tell you, then, that the "stars of evening" are a snare. "Sunset" is full of peril, but the moon, whether "pale," "eerie," "elfin," "silver," "sailing," "hung," "crescent," or "full" is fatal. Never write a line about the moon. Beware of "harvest" and the whole circle of thought that surrounds it. "Sheaves" are treacherous. The following words, and several hundred more like them, I would suggest that you leave severely alone unless you can use them in new connections and as they were never used before: "serried," "somber," "weird," "solace," "leash," "morose," to say nothing of "dreary" and "weary." "Cypress trees" are bad. The "hoot of an owl" is terrible, especially if it is "an ominous hoot." Beware of "moaning winds." "Balmy breezes" are poison. "Zephyrs" are all of that. "Brooks," whether they "babble" or "ripple" or "flash" or "sing," are no good. "Fireflies" and "nightingales" are risky to monkey with. (Recently I read a charming set of verses, for children, on "Goldfish"! Now that's something!)

Unless you are a strong swimmer, don't go near the water. I mean the sea. Some poets have drowned in it, versifiers are almost sure to. Your sea is likely to be "troubled" or "placid" or "heaving foam." And don't be struck by "nameless fears." Don't let your soul get "flooded with holy calm." Don't get "flooded" with anything. Keep your feet down and your head up, but be careful to look where you are going. The "starry firmament" is a bad guide, and you might also entertain proper horror for "boundless space."

A "child's gay laugh" is painful. Something should be done about "merry children." If they have "angel faces," hanging is too good for them. "Smiling through tears" is no way to conduct oneself any more. You see, the point of all this has been well put by a modern writer whom some persons would call a poet, Mr. Allen Upward. I don't know who the Emperor Han was, but Mr. Upward relates of him that the first time he heard a certain word he said, "It is strange." The second time, he said, "It is divine." The third time, he said, "Let the speaker be put to death." It is certain that words grow shabby, while phrases actually die and should be buried.

Let me tell you, too, now that I have my hand upon your shoulder, that there are worn-out rhymes, lots of them. There are rhymes that are too facile; almost all rhymes ending in open "e" are cheap, such as "sea" and "lea," but that is not all that is the matter with a word like "lea." When "emperor" was first rhymed with "floor," the Emperor Han might have been pleased. Now we are getting a little tired of that kind of rhyming. Above all, see that you don't "pull" things like this—"gardens fair," "beauty rare." Twenty years ago we all did this with impunity, but that was before Miss Harriet Monroe came along and set the house of English poetry in order.

I suggest that you write simple four-line stanzas and try to rhyme the first line with the third, the second with the fourth. This form will do you for a long time to come. I counsel you to avoid tricky forms. If you ever write acrostics I shall do my best to have you boiled in oil. If you celebrate the death of a friend, or a Mother Superior, in a rondeau or a sonnet, I shall deliver you to the torturers with a recommendation that they pass you on to the executioner. Even though your pastor be arrived at what is called his Sacerdotal Golden Jubilee, keep your mouth shut: don't sing a note. Leave it to the choir, they have been practicing a new Mass for the occasion, and that is enough.

Writing verse about the helpless dead is one of the strongest arguments I know against the theory and especially the practice of evolution. I knew a good priest, but a bad poet, who was addicted to this. He no sooner learned of a death in the wide circle of his friends and acquaintances than he was there, on deck, so to speak, with a poem. He became a poetical undertaker, wrapping the dead in iambic winding sheets. Like the trumpet to the warhorse, or the gong to the firehorse, death was a signal and a summons and a challenge to his "Pegasus," as he would call it. One of his living friends, who was at the time not so very well, declared that this elegist had added a new terror to death.

A good deal of what passes for poetry is really only eloquence, rhetoric. I suppose it is impossible to settle by definition the boundary line between rhetoric and poetry. One man's poetry is another man's rhetoric, and vice versa: indeed, what is vice to one may be verse to another. But I have one way of judging, to my own satisfaction, at least. The spurious and the genuine in pictures usually look differently when hung together—counterfeit money has a different ring from that of good coin. The thing to do, then, is to bring them together and test one by the other.

You might look here, as Hamlet says, "On this picture, and on this." The first speaks of sunset on a ship coming in from sea:

> The sunset pageant in the West
> has filled your canvas curves with rose
> and jeweled every toppling crest
> that crashes into silver snows.

The second runs as follows:

> Why does the evening always wear
> a white-rose moon in her star-grey hair?

In my opinion, the first of these is rhetoric, the second is poetry The first sounds fine, it is eloquent, and until one analyzes it, seems true. It is one of those glowing things, but I believe that it has a false glow. Let us see. In the first place, it is not the sunset "as pageant" which fills the ship's sails with color. In the second place, the phrase "in the West" serves merely to complete the line and achieve rhyme, without adding anything to the thought. "Canvas curves" is a typical rhetorical expression. It means sails. One wonders why "sails" was not used with an appropriate epithet which might add to the picture as well as the length of the line. In the third line this "pageant" which has filled the sails with rose has "jeweled" the waves. Now there is no good reason why a wave should be "jeweled." What are the "silver snows" in the poet's mind here? Presumably, foam. So it goes, and, mind you, this is a stanza from the work of a real poet, from the greenwood, so to speak.

Another point, when the rhetorician gets through his work, his words are static and dead. They do not go on working. This is a highly important difference, I think. The rhetoric one finds in verse seems satisfied to resound. It states glowingly, eloquently. In poetry, the words are alive and forever operative. They suggest rains of thought, they lead on dreams, they are productive. (There is poetry which is actually generative of poetry.) This is altogether apart from the beauty, simple or splendid, which they may possess in their collocation.

The couplet cited above I believe exemplifies all this. I could rake the great poets and the standard collections of poetry and find innumerable examples for you. It happens that the two lines cited here are the work of a college poet. It would be well if all young poets used their eyes and their fancy to such good effect as he did. We might then have poetry fresh and young written by poets who are young and fresh in the right sense, instead of chunks of rhetoric such as "the vasty reaches of the Western plain." We might even have, every decade or so, a nice new phrase about the moon.

The aim to be brief is on the whole a commendable one. Young writers are inclined to be diffuse, to spread their material thin. In the effort to be brief one may cut to the quick. The result is verse that is clipped as close as a convict's head. A good example of this bad effect is the following:

On throne of gold
sat regent bold:
at beck of thine
they figure twine.

This writer might have given himself a little more elbow room in which to work.

Finally, there is another defect, I suppose a psychological one. It is the poetry that we have come to know as "cerebral." I don't know how to describe it for you except to say it is ingrown thinking, which means pressed outward, it turns in on itself and gets imbedded in the brain. Young poets often have this difficulty of expression, but not young poets alone. It is sometimes an infirmity of noble minds. I should say that the following is an example of the cerebral style of poetry:

> You blazon me with jeweled insignia.
> A flaming nebula
> rims in my life. And yet
> you set
> the word upon me, unconfessed,
> to go unguessed.

All this has been frightfully negative and I suppose discouraging too. You might reasonably say with Charles lamb that I have told you "what to don't," not what to do. Only the broadest directions will have any value. You must use your own senses, do your own seeing, smelling, tasting, hearing, etc., and you must read poetry, plenty of it. Take, for example, these lines of Coleridge:

> There is not wind enough to twirl
> the one red leaf, the last of its clan,
> that dances as often as dance it can,
> hanging so light and hanging so high,
> on the topmost twig that looks up at the sky.

You might repeat that to yourself—about seventy-five times a day will do. Test other poetry by it, to see if it has the right *ring*. Consider Shakespeare:

> Daffodils,
> that come before the swallow dares, and take
> the winds of March with beauty.

It will not be necessary for you, however, to confine your reading to the great poets of the past. A lady named Rose O'Neill, of our own time, has written these lines:

> Few there are who live, alas!
> and they are far from here,
> who know how young and dear I was

when I was young and dear.

Compare that with the cerebral verse above and with the rhetorical "canvas curves."

In advising you to use your own eyes I have the hope that you may give us an image like the following:

Tulips are tripping down the path.

You might make an artistic retreat of a day or so meditating on the choice and use of adjectives in Mrs. Aline Kilmer's single poem "Candles that Burn." While you are at it, why not consider Emily Dickinson when she affirms in a poem on autumn "the rose is out of town" and also,

Softly through the altered air
hurries a timid leaf.

This same interesting poet wrote:

The robins stand as thick today
as flakes of snow stood yesterday.

I suppose your textbook would list this as a hyperbole, but it is a rather nice way, don't you think, of putting things?

At the start of this letter, if you can remember back so far, I believe I said I had no intention of pointing out the pitfalls that lie in wait for you, and now at the close I find I have done little else. This waywardness you will recognize at once as a family trait. Could the Irish have been a great race if they had held themselves in all things to a rigid consistency? Having made this harmless inquiry, I pause for a reply,

Your exhausted uncle,
Christopher [Charles O'Donnell]

Index of Titles

Index of First Lines